D1356141

Counterturbulence Marketing

COUNTERTURBULENCE MARKETING

A Proactive Strategy for
Volatile
Economic Times

A. COSKUN SAMLI

Quorum Books
Westport, Connecticut • London

Library of Congress Cataloging-in-Publication Data

Samli, A. Coskun.
   Counterturbulence marketing : a proactive strategy for volatile
economic times / A. Coskun Samli.
     p. cm.
   Includes bibliographical references and index.
   ISBN 0–89930–796–5 (alk. paper)
   1. Marketing—Management. I. Title.
HF5415.13.S238 1993
658.8—dc20   93–19116

British Library Cataloguing in Publication Data is available.

Library of Congress Catalog Card Number: 93–19116
ISBN: 0–89930–796–5

First published in 1993

Quorum Books, 88 Post Road West, Westport, CT 06881
An imprint of Greenwood Publishing Group, Inc.

Printed in the United States of America

The paper used in this book complies with the
Permanent Paper Standard issued by the National
Information Standards Organization (Z39.48–1984).

10 9 8 7 6 5 4 3 2 1

This book is dedicated to Bea and others like her
who do their utmost to deliver value to their clients.
Their efforts make ours the best marketing system in the world.

Contents

Exhibits

Preface

During my long career, I have seen many booms and many recessions. I have observed and studied many long range trends. And above all I have experienced hundreds upon hundreds of firms entering the market and then failing or discontinuing. Thus, I truly believe that turbulence in the marketplace is an ongoing phenomenon. It cannot be eliminated. It can be predicted only partially, if at all. The only solution for turbulence in the marketplace, which is caused by many short and long term factors, is proactivity.

This book is about proactive marketing. In a dynamic market the firm cannot function with some static financial processes alone. There are those who think that markets cannot be influenced. The firms that must be inactive and coast are likely to fail first. Those firms that react to market conditions but allow much time to lapse are the second group to fail. Only those firms that are proactive and swift in their actions survive the severest turbulent impact. They even benefit from the conditions that are causing the turbulence.

Exhibit P-1 illustrates the basic premise of this book. Two groups of factors — short-run and long-run — create the turbulence in the marketplace. This turbulence forces the firm to discontinue or to fail unless it takes a counterturbulence posture. This counterturbulence position can be obtained by being proactive, that is, anticipating, reading the early indicators, moving fast to counteract changes, and monitor the total process very closely. Proactive marketing, by definition, enhances the firm's probability to survive and prosper.

Exhibit P-1
Market Turbulence versus Proactivity

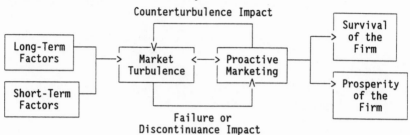

This Preface presents the key elements of proactive thinking and proactive marketing.

Chapter 1 describes some of the key short-run and long-run factors that are causing turbulence. The list presented in this chapter is limited; however, it illustrates how these factors interact with the marketplace.

Chapter 2 presents a discussion of some of the trends in business population. Here again, a distinction is made between the short-run and long-run business trends.

Chapter 3 argues that the cost of turbulence is very high. An attempt is made here to distinguish between direct and indirect costs and implies that firms are managed by a bottom line instead of for a bottom line. It posits that this type of reactive behavior is not only detrimental to the firm but also to the economy as a whole.

Chapter 4 argues that the firms have to move away from catering only to stockholders and cater also to stakeholders. This is a key point in a proactive mode. The chapter also discusses the inactive, reactive, and proactive modes of marketing management.

Chapter 5 points out that one of the most important features of proactive marketing is detecting early signals in the marketplace. Marketing symptomatology must be perfectly functional so that the firm can have an early counterturbulence posture.

Chapter 6 delves into developing new products and adjusting the existing ones based on procedures established by proactive marketing management plans.

Chapter 7 examines pricing strategies. It establishes pricing parameters that would enhance the firm's ability to survive in turbulent times.

Chapter 8 looks into the promotional aspects of proactive marketing. I take the position that basic promotional activity must change quickly as different types of turbulence enter the marketplace.

Chapter 9 claims that proactive marketing generates and maintains customer loyalty. It enhances the concept that without customer loyalty the firm cannot survive adversities of market turbulence.

Chapter 10 explores some of the most important logistics issues and the application of total quality management (TQM) to marketing. Most recent value-added developments in logistics are used to enhance customer satisfaction and, therefore, customer loyalty.

Chapter 11 makes the point that in order to keep the customers happy and loyal, it is necessary to understand the changes in the marketplace. The firm must detect the changes in its market segments and then must try to customize its services to satisfy these changing targets. Similarly a discussion is presented on the emerging new market segments.

Chapter 12 puts together the *value marketing* model to cope with turbulence. This model presents marketing proactivity at its best.

Finally, the Epilogue puts forth a research agenda to improve proactive marketing process and its ability to cope with market turbulence.

Acknowledgments

Many people have contributed directly or indirectly to the development of this book. Early on, my thinking was formed by the dissertation I wrote under the meticulous guidance of Professor Stanley Hollander, who is my mentor, friend, and one of the best scholars I know. His thoughts and his impact on me have been spectacular.

My friend, colleague, and co-author of many years, professor Joe Sirgy, always has been available to argue or interact. His influence on my thinking has been profound.

My other colleagues at the University of North Florida knowingly or unknowingly have been pulled into many discussions pertaining to various points in this book. Professor Tansu Barker has played a critical role in the development of Chapter 5. I am particularly grateful to Professor Zabriskie whose thinking was uniquely important in developing Chapter 6.

My friend Keith Goldsmith of Customized Transportation, Inc. (CTI) was kind enough to read Chapter 10 and make some important suggestions. My dean, Ed Johnson, and my department head, Robert Pickhardt, were kind enough to give me support and encouragement so that I could produce this volume.

This book could not have been written without the research help received from my graduate assistant, Riaz M. Abdul. He has developed his research skills to the point that I had outstanding support for all the chapters in this book.

Our secretaries, Jane Wood and Betty Geitz, were always there to help. However, nobody's contribution has been as great as that of my secretary, Leanna Payne, who not only typed from my hardly legible handwritten notes but also carefully read every word in every chapter. At times she even gave me her seal of approval, which I value very highly.

Hundreds of my graduate students listened, reacted, argued, and even disagreed with me about many points that are made in this book. They were patient enough to listen to my, at times, rather out of the ordinary ideas. I owe them much. Beverly Chapman gave me a helping hand in editing the book. Finally, Bea Goldsmith read, argued, and advised me on many parts of this book. Her contributions are quite visible in many parts of this volume.

To these and many other people who over the years, discussed, interacted, or researched these issues with me, I extend my deep gratitude. I, however, am solely responsible for the contents of this book. I certainly hope that it makes a modest but noticeable contribution to the well-being of all of my friends, known and unknown, in business.

Counterturbulence Marketing

Introduction

This book, above all, is about proactive marketing; we could also say dynamic marketing. Proactive marketing implies that the firm does not simply believe that market conditions can be significantly altered or directly influenced. Instead, the firm functions to keep ahead of market changes and market developments in such a way that it will not only survive but also prosper.

This behavior must be distinguished from reactive and inactive behaviors that imply that the firm does not pay much attention to the possibility of counteracting market adversities. Furthermore, it does not even believe that it can actually do something about the market changes. Hence it takes a fatalistic point of view of doing nothing. This behavior describes inactive marketing (Samli, 1992).

This book is also about turbulence, it is about counterturbulence, it is about survival in the marketplace, and it is focused on *value marketing*. It is posited here that the firm can survive turbulence and even prosper from it by developing an effective *value marketing plan*.

Some years ago Peter Drucker (1980) stated: "A time of turbulence is a dangerous time, but its greatest danger is a temptation to deny reality. ... The most dangerous turbulence today results from the collision between the delusions of the decision makers" (4). He went on to say: "But a time of turbulence is also one of great opportunity for those who can understand, accept and exploit the new realities. It is above all a time of opportunity for leadership" (5).

It has been over 13 years since these thoughts were put forth. Turbulence today is more noticeable and more dangerous. Collision (both implicit and explicit) among the decision makers is also more noticeable. Firms are all cutting down expenses and downsizing. Similarly, opportunities are perhaps greater or at least as great and not quite so well tapped.

In a recent recession (1991–1992) and in earlier recessions of the 1980s, management, in a sense, denied reality. Firms tried to rectify the problem by financial austerity programs. Companies scaled the operations and downsized.

This book posits that a proactive marketing plan can be a true counterturbulence weapon. This, I believe, is what Drucker articulates as understanding, accepting, and exploiting the new realities. A proactive marketing plan cannot be constructed and put in place functionally without understanding, accepting, and exploiting the new realities that are already in place in the economy, or at least emerging.

The proactive marketing plan is termed *value marketing*, which is quite similar to recent concepts such as *relationship marketing* or *interactive marketing*. It is seen to be not just satisfying the customers' needs but providing as much value as possible so that they will be delighted and stay with the company. With the strong backing of its customers the firm can weather any kind of turbulence. However, providing satisfaction for the customer is not a simple task. The emerging or prevailing turbulence in a dynamic market causes significant changes in the customer's needs, wants, and desires and may even change the customers themselves. Thus, developing a proactive marketing plan such as value marketing is not enough. A continuing support process must regularly re-shape, adjust, delete, and innovate the specifics of the value marketing plan and its implementation.

The continuing support process must be ongoing and intact so that critical changes that the proactive marketing plan introduced can be further adjusted. Hopefully, this will keep ahead of turbulence, which is the crux of counterturbulence marketing.

Because the proactive marketing plan is called value marketing, the support process is called value marketing support process. This simple interrelationship is depicted in Exhibit I-1. Turbulence forces the firm to develop a value marketing plan, and this plan receives ammunition constantly from the support process.

Thus, counterturbulence marketing has two equally important and totally interdependent components: a value marketing plan and a value marketing support process. Whereas the proactive value marketing plan is

Exhibit I-1
The Essence of Counterturbulence Marketing

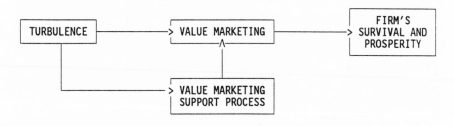

constructed, implemented, and periodically adjusted the support process must be continuous. This book reflects these two key components.

In order to understand and operationalize the total concept of counter-turbulence marketing there must be a major change in the management's attitude. Management, in Drucker's terms, must not ignore the realities of the market; rather, it must understand and work with them. This is not only a change in the mind set but also a switch from traditional to new realities. The switch from traditions is related to the recent management era beginning with the 1980s and continuing to the present. This particular era is reflected by managing by a bottom line rather than managing for a bottom line. The recent tradition in management has been a questionable focus on financial management.

This book proposes that, in order to survive in the dynamic, turbulent, and unpredictable marketplace, the firm must manage external uncontrollables by proactive marketing measures. Finances are a measure of performance but not quite a means to an end. The firm must do what it must do *for a bottom line* by managing well a value marketing program.

Therefore, although the supporting process of value marketing may not be seen to be financially sound in the short run, without this process the firm may not survive in the long run. Thus, once again the firm must not be managed by a bottom line but for a bottom line. This management goal, in turbulent times, may mean survival. The firm must survive in order to prosper.

Most of this book deals with the elements in the total support process. First, without this support process there is no counterturbulence marketing and, second, the key elements of the value marketing plan are based on this support system. Without this interactive nature of the value marketing plan and the value marketing support process there is no counterturbulence. Thus, counterturbulence marketing is composed of two key elements, but these two are intertwined and cannot be separated.

One final note: this book does not just dwell upon customer satisfaction; it attempts to show how to provide the customer with as much value as possible. This means that the firm does not think of its own existence and its own survival only, but about the society and the economy as well. It is, therefore, proposed here that value marketing prevents the firm from being harmed, and, simultaneously, it benefits the society as well. Therein lies the true value of constructive, creative, and *value adding marketing management*. All of these lead to proactivity and counterturbulence.

When we understand turbulence and its impact on the firm as well as the need for proactive marketing, we will have more creative ideas regarding the firm and its customers. I believe, however, that this is the beginning of a new era of managerial orientation toward coping with turbulence. The key concept is *counterturbulence marketing*.

REFERENCES

Drucker, Peter F. 1980. *Managing in Turbulent Times*. New York: Harper & Row.
Samli, A. Coskun. 1992. *Social Responsibility in Marketing*. Westport, CT: Quorum Books.

1

Turbulent Times and Turbulent Markets

INTRODUCTION

Marketing takes place in the economy. It either moves along with currents of economic activity or moves against the economic tide. These two options for marketing, that is, pro or counter economic tide, are not of equal importance. Their outcomes are not likely to be equal. Marketing as a powerful process and socioeconomic force must be proactive enough to decide which is the most desirable choice and must proceed accordingly. If the economic tide is low, marketing needs to go against the tide so that overall economic activity is heightened. If the economic tide is high, proactive marketing may pull back and even be engaged in demarketing so that the economy will not enter a hyperinflationary era. The high and low tides in the economy are part of the turbulence that exists in modern markets.

This chapter explores turbulent conditions in the economy, their causes, and the challenges for proactive marketing. The challenge particularly reflects itself in terms of the changes in the quality of life (QOL).

CAUSES OF TURBULENCE

In discussing turbulence, Drucker says: "Turbulence, by definition, is irregular, non-linear, erratic. But its underlying causes can be analyzed, predicted, managed." (1989, 2). A major portion of this chapter is devoted to exploring this concept.

Underlying causes of economic irregularities that are coined as turbulence can be classified into two major categories: short-run and long-run.

Causes of turbulence in the short run can be further classified in the form of business cycles and a number of other temporary and sudden changes.

Business Cycles

There are pervasive and persistent nonseasonal fluctuations in modern capitalist economies (Zarnowitz, 1990) that have very deep and far-reaching implications. When the economy is in a downturn, the cost to society is immense. This cost to society is even greater when marketing is considered. The unemployment created by a business cycle means very large sums of lost purchasing power. Thus, because of the lost volumes of sales, while marketing losses very large rewards in the form of profits, consumers also suffer a distinct and acute decline in their quality of life. Business cycles have been recurrent but not periodic (Zarnowitz, 1990). During these cycles there are diverse economic and non-economic processes that become widely diffused and synchronized to create major fluctuations in the economy in terms of total output, employment, real income, and real sales (Zarnowitz, 1990). During these upturns and downturns many economic and social activities move in the same direction, and their motions and intensity overlap. Thus, the impact of these business cycles is felt widely and simultaneously by almost the whole society. Their immediate impact is felt in decreasing profits, increasing unemployment, and a serious deterioration in consumer confi-dence. The immediate impact sends out short-run shock waves in terms of further reduced business and consumer and government expenditures. The decreased spending on the part of business, consumer, and government sectors automatically takes the economy to lower plateaus of equilibrium where the immediate tendency to change is very low. Thus, in addition to immediate, deep, and far-reaching impact, business cycles, in this sense, can be much longer lasting than many people expect them to be.

In addition to decreasing purchasing power and willingness to buy, which have a devastating impact on marketing, the tendency on the part of the business sector to cut down business expenditures (which is erroneously called fiscal responsibility) will have further devastating impact on marketing. The latter stems from the fact that many business expenditures such as promotional, sales, and market research outlays are cut first. This is because they do not show tangible and immediate results. A financially driven management with up-front bottom line orientation would consider expenditures with intangible results to be dead weights on the well-being of the firm. Therefore, these expenditures are likely to be cut further as the business cycle progresses. Because of the declining marketing activity, the firm's market position becomes progressively worse. Sales go down, profits shrink, and returns on investments approach zero. Thus, the *conventional wisdom* of non-marketing managements in turbulent times contributes substantially to the turbulence itself.

Other Temporary and Sudden Changes

Short-term economic turbulence is also caused by sudden jolts prompted by some unexpected events. At least twice in the mid- and late-1970s oil prices were raised by the Organization of Petroleum Exporting Countries (OPEC) through an embargo, and oil became scarce in such a way that the economic impact was a partial or full-fledged recession. Other sudden changes, such as stopping a large wheat sale to Russia or major changes in military spending, would cause a sudden shock that, in turn, would start the recession (or the business cycle). There may be many such unexpected events that would either start the recession or deepen it. In either case the impact on marketing is borderline devastation. As the recession begins and progresses, marketing's overall position deteriorates progressively.

One of the more commonly articulated temporary and sudden changes is related to politics. There are two versions of this theory. First, is the Nordhaus electoral model (1975) that purports that the party in power manipulates the economy to win elections; second is the Hibbs partisan model (1977) that maintains that macropolicies of one party as opposed to the other would induce a recession. Although these points are argued back and forth, it is clear that there is some evidence of politically induced business cycles (Haynes & Stone, 1990).

In addition to the short-run causes of turbulence, there are numerous major trends in the U.S. economy. These trends are creating different types of turbulence which are, individually or jointly, making day-to-day business activities difficult at best and almost futile at worst.

LONG-RUN CAUSES OF TURBULENCE

There are at least seven long-term trends that are causing turbulence in the United States and providing tremendous challenges to marketing.

These are: (1) change in competition-increasing oligopoly; (2) movement from production to information; (3) foreign competition; (4) changing power structure; (5) changing life styles and consumer behavior; (6) political impact; and (7) downsizing — rightsizing or wrongsizing.

Change in Competition-Increasing Oligopoly

During the 1980s and early 1990s a merger frenzy swept the United States. Leveraged buyouts and unfriendly takeovers during that period were so excessive that almost all of the major industries moved in the direction of fewer and larger companies (Samli, 1992). As the firms become more oligopolistic, they are further removed from consumers and the market. With newly acquired power, they are capable of keeping prices high, research and production expenses low, and reducing the middle management by layoffs. They cut down their promotional expenditures and efforts to compete because competition is not that critical any more.

The merger activity is still accelerating — not in terms of numbers of firms involved, but their total value. While in 1980 there were only 94 mergers (out of 1,889 total), with a value of over $1 million, by 1988 this had gone up to 369 mergers. Similarly, while in 1980 there were four mergers with a value of over $1 billion, this number had risen to 45 in 1988 (Weston and Chung, 1990). The increasing size of mergers and acquisitions indicates an increasing oligopolistic tendency in U.S. economy. Exhibit 1-1 illustrates this situation by pointing out the increasing total market share of the top five firms in three industries. As can be seen, primarily through merger and acquisition, in these industries

Exhibit 1-1
Increasing Oligopolies

(in percent)

Industry	Total Share of Top Five Firms 1985	Total Share of Top Five Firms 1990
Appliances	79.8	97.4
Tires	57.6	66.1
Software	55.6	61.9

Source: Adapted from Samli, A. Coskun. 1992. *Social Responsibility in Marketing*. Westport, CT: Quorum Books.

the market share of the top five firms increased substantially in such a short period as five years. These industries are typical rather than being exceptions.

Movement from Production to Information

The U.S. economy is changing radically. Perhaps one of the most important changes is related to the movement from being a manufacturing and production economy to generating and disseminating information and emphasizing services more readily. Moving from manufacturing to information and services creates a major change in income distribution. Information industries are relatively less labor intensive than manufacturing, with larger disparities between the top and bottom pay scales.

Naisbitt (1982) stated that the number of information workers in the United States increased from approximately 17 percent in 1950 to more than 60 percent in the early 1980s. What he calls information jobs includes programmers, teachers, clerks, secretaries, accountants, stock brokers, managers, insurance people, bureaucrats, lawyers, bankers, and technicians. Additionally, even in manufacturing firms many hold information jobs. He concludes by indicating that "most Americans spend their time creating, processing, or distributing information" (14).

The transition of U.S. society from a production to an information economy creates serious turbulence. During the transitionary period there is joblessness. Many workers are displaced and are jobless until new skills are acquired and new jobs are created. In the meantime, there may be critical hardship on thousands of workers because of job loss and income loss. Furthermore, critical new income distribution patterns emerge. All of these changes have significant impacts on the economy and marketing. Not only the traditional ways of performing the marketing process may need to be revised but also some of the older ways of marketing may even go against the changes and be quite counterproductive. Furthermore, joblessness in some circles and newly found wealth in others puts substantial pressure on the marketing system to change and to adjust quickly. Marketing of information is likely to be quite different than marketing of manufactured products. Similarly, changing income distribution prompted by the movement from production to information changes consumption patterns and life styles and targets audiences that are all very critical for marketing.

Foreign Competition

Naisbitt and Aburdene (1990) discuss the emergence of a global boom in the 1990s. Although internationalization of markets for goods and services has significant benefits, it also has devastating effects on some local economies. As this book is being written, GM has announced laying off 74,000 workers. Although Japanese and Korean cars provide benefits for the U.S. consumer, their sudden competitive upsurge has been nearly devastating to some local single industry economies in the United States. These local economies, in the past, heavily depended on the auto industry and now are depressed.

Changing Power Structure

Samli (1992) distinguishes two different democracies: political and economic. Whereas political democracy is one-person-one-vote, economic democracy is one-dollar-one-vote. He maintains that unless these two democracies are checking and balancing each other the society will not be able to optimize its economic efforts.

From 1977 through 1988 the after-tax average income of the poorest one-fifth of U.S. households fell 10 percent after adjusting for inflation (Shapiro & Greenstein, 1991). By contrast, the top one-fifth of households experienced an average gain of 34 percent in their after-tax income adjusted for inflation. During the same period, the richest 1 percent of U.S. citizens received an increase of 122 percent in their after-tax income, again adjusted for inflation (Shapiro & Greenstein, 1991).

Thus, economic power is becoming more and more concentrated in the hands of a few. This trend, in conjunction with the tendency of having more oligopolies in the industry, is causing a dramatic change in the power structure of U.S. markets. The change in the power structure is creating an ever widening gap between the two democracies. The widening gap between economic and political democracies is taking away the opportunity from certain consumers to enjoy equal footing with the rest of the society in all areas of consumption (Samli, 1992). Certain consumer groups that are more vulnerable in terms of their economic power, education, or decision making capabilities become continually worse off. Additionally, the need and demand for certain goods and services in the society become more lopsided in favor of more and more concentrated economic power, thus, leaving the vulnerable consumer groups with fewer and fewer products and services to choose from and to purchase.

The widening gap between the two democracies is virtually eliminating any existing checks and balances that will bring the two democracies together and restore equal opportunity for consumers to improve the quality of life for all (Samli, 1992). The imbalance between the two democracies is making economic democracy more important. As it becomes more powerful it starts influencing political democracy more and more. This process accelerates the concentration of power. This whole situation causes turbulence for marketing.

Changing Life Styles and Consumer Behavior

During the past two decades there have been many important changes in U.S. consumers' life styles and purchase behaviors. These trends will continue emerging, changing, and discontinuing. Increasing consumer sophistication and new technology, along with the changing economic status and consumer values, are causing the emergence of new consumer groups and pressing for the emergence, change, or discontinuation of many products and services (Michman, 1991).

Consumers' increasing health consciousness is making a critical dent both in pre-prepared foods as well as fast foods. After more than four decades McDonald's has changed its standard menu in order to provide a more healthy menu. Consumption of vitamins and food supplements is at an all time high.

Many products are disappearing, particularly those that are expensive, bulky, or energy inefficient. Environmental concerns and impact of Greenpeace is causing the emergence of many new products and the demise of others.

Direct marketing and telemarketing are changing buying behaviors and purchasing patterns. The variety of products purchased through these processes is constantly varying.

During the 1980s the lower 20 percent of the population lost 10 percent of their real income after taxes. The middle 20 percent barely maintained their income. This picture particularly worsened in the latter part of the 1980s and early 1990s (Phillips, 1991; Shapiro & Greenstein, 1991). The impact of this deterioration affected many consumer durable products as well as the housing market. These industries suffered a steadily deteriorating trend. As new homes are not purchased, U.S. nuclear families become extended families. These changes have made a significant impact on consumption of durable and non-durable goods. As families live together under the same roof, emphasis is on purchasing consumer durables. Families share these expensive items. Furthermore, there is no room in the household for multiple consumer non-durables. Households will purchase a lot more foods, health items, and other consumer non-durables.

From these few and sketchy examples, it can be seen that marketing is influenced very noticeably by these changes and developments.

Political Impact

In addition to the earlier discussion about political parties causing their own business cycles, there are other political impacts. The joint political policies of Reagan and Bush have given a great boost to military-related industries. These industries, unlike typical manufacturing, have some type of elitist orientation to employment. They employ a few scientists and select workers and pay very highly. This trend, if continued, exacerbates the lopsided distribution of income. During the same era, deregulation policies reduced competition by encouraging leveraged buyouts and unfriendly takeovers. Thus, this political climate created turbulence in the economy. As competition decreased or changed, marketing activities changed even more dramatically.

Downsizing, Rightsizing, or Wrongsizing

During the past decade, downsizing, a new concept, changed the organizational structure of U.S. businesses. Subsequently, it was renamed rightsizing.

The basic premise of downsizing or rightsizing is that, over the years, U.S. firms created too many organizational layers that created too much of a bureaucracy and, therefore, inflexibility. In the meantime, the Japanese success in the world markets has made it noticeable that the Japanese basically have fatter and shallower organizational structures. They do not have the U.S. pyramid where multiple layers depict the organizational structure with one chief executive officer (CEO) or president on top. The Japanese organizational structure is flat and rectangular. It is composed of multiple groups and offers very little opportunity for upward mobility.

As U.S. companies started downsizing (rightsizing), some 2,000 middle managers lost their jobs daily for a number of years. This situation has been (and is) causing substantial turbulence. As many lose their jobs, morale in U.S. offices is just about at an all-time low, and productivity is deteriorating. Additionally, many organizations are finding themselves without certain skills. Typically, personnel divisions are firing the people, and strategic planning and administrations, after the fact, are realizing that they are short of certain skills. In some cases, companies are short of important skills that would enable them to survive in the marketplace, and, hence, their market performance is becoming worse even though they are cutting costs by trimming the management (Tomasco, 1990). In this process many marketing personnel were laid off and many of their functions were eliminated. Thus, the situation is basically accelerating the turbulence. This turbulence has led to a 12-year recession.

A 12-YEAR RECESSION

The recession that started in the U.S. economy between 1979 and 1980 has been going strong while this book is being written in 1992. During this period, our economy performed quite badly so that many business specialists, economists, and social thinkers have either warned us about continuing low growth (Ohmae, 1982) or they have interpreted low growth as the new reality of the economic environment (Drucker, 1989). Although recessions are considered to be short-run phenomena, the overall U.S. economic performance during that period can be considered as a prolonged recession with additional troughs and a few peaks. The performance of this mighty economy has been so poor that it is almost a testimonial for the late Lord Keynes' concept of sub-optimal equilibrium. He argues that, left alone, the economy in recession or depression can adjust itself to a less-than-satisfactory performance level without any immediate tendency to change (Keynes, 1936).

Ohmae (1982) discusses five specific new economic facts, or realities, that are reinforcing or prolonging this 12-year business cycle. These new economic facts are: (1) continuing low growth, (2) market maturity and strategic stalemate, (3) uneven distribution of resources, (4) growing international complexities, and (5) irreversible inflation.

As far as Ohmae is concerned, continuing low growth limits the margin of error in managers' decisions and narrows the leeway within which mistakes can be overlooked or rectified. The market becomes more unforgiving. Management starts foregoing risk taking entrepreneurial activities and becomes more involved in financial manipulations as a means for growth and survival. However, financial manipulations are not likely to provide the economy with a healthy growth rate. Much of the financial manipulations in the 1980s have been by corporate raiders who aimed their activities toward relatively smaller and profitable firms. These firms were acquired through unfriendly takeovers (UTOs) and leveraged buyouts (LBOs). They were broken into components and sold for a profit. In this whole process the U.S. economy suffered in two distinct ways. First, the best and most efficient companies were purchased and dissected; hence, they lost the synergism which took many years to build. Second, as UTOs and LBOs continued, the country's financial resources as well as research and development (R&D) resources were tied up by these major financial manipulations and, hence, turbulence became worse.

Market maturity and strategic stalemate are caused by a self-fulfilling prophecy of if the market is not growing, the corporate entity will not be investing in advance of market growth. It will, therefore, eliminate risk and, by definition, reduce the growth prospects in the economy. It is quite likely that all participating corporate entities will take a similar strategic position and create a stalemate of economic non-growth, non-changing market shares in an overall stabilized market share picture by all participants.

Uneven distribution of resources, perhaps, relates to the fact that companies, as they consider allocation of investments, tend to be bureaucratic without paying attention to the overall balance of the company's business portfolio (Ohmae, 1982). They are not capable of developing what Drucker (1989) termed an "opportunity budget" and invest accordingly.

Growing international complexities are reflected in companies' being forced to revise global business in the form of multilocal. Modern multinational corporations do not have the original notion of "buy raw materials wherever they are cheapest, manufacture wherever wages are lowest, and sell wherever the products will bring the highest price" (Ohmae, 1982, 179). Instead, modern multinational companies are catering to local needs of local markets accordingly. The world is becoming more fragmented and cannot be treated as a single homogeneous unit. Thus, overseas competition and overseas opportunities are becoming more difficult and more costly to cope with or take advantage of.

Irreversible inflation, in Ohmae's point of view, is an ongoing activity. Inflation cannot be reversed unless a costly unemployment strategy is employed. Continuing inflation, he maintains, has a dulling effect on entrepreneurial spirit and on almost the whole economy.

Thus, the five economic realities put forth by Ohmae have contributed to as well as reinforced the low performance level of U.S. economy. This low level of performance can be seen as the outcome of the economic turbulence.

The turbulence and the forces causing it are directly and indirectly impacting the quality of life (QOL) in this society. This relationship is discussed briefly in the following section.

RELATIONSHIP BETWEEN ECONOMIC TURBULENCE AND QUALITY OF LIFE

Economic turbulence has a close relationship with the QOL. This relationship is depicted in Exhibit 1-2. The exhibit illustrates a circular chain reaction. Short-run and long-run factors cause economic turbulence. This turbulence, in turn, causes a more cautious behavior on the part of business, government, and consumers. All three groups are decreasing their spending under the guise of fiscal responsibility. Decreasing spending causes a decline in both production and consumption. The inevitable impact of these declines is a reduction in existing high paying jobs and an increase in unemployment. All of these developments further refuel the already turbulent economic environment.

Exhibit 1-2
The Relationship between Economic Turbulence and the Quality of Life

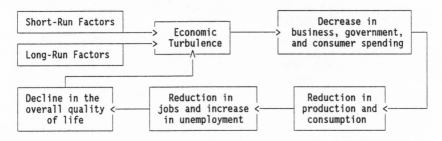

As seen in Exhibit 1-2, the whole process is circular and self-feeding. The implication of this feature is that, once started, the process could continue indefinitely, causing a general deterioration in the economic well-being and the quality of life which are prevailing in the society

SUMMARY

This chapter presents a discussion relating to turbulence in the economy. It is proposed that turbulence, which is caused by a number of short-term and long-term factors, causes a decline in the economic well-being of the society and the quality of life. Among the short-term factors are business cycles and other temporary sudden changes.

There are at least seven long-term factors causing turbulence. They are: (1) change in competition, (2) movement from production to information, (3) foreign competition, (4) changing power structure, (5) changing life styles, (6) political impacts, and (7) downsizing.

The turbulence has caused a 12-year recession that, in turn, created new economic realities. These appear to be reinforcing this prolonged business cycle.

REFERENCES

Drucker, Peter. 1989. *The New Realities*. New York: Harper & Row.

Haynes, Stephen E., and Joe A. Stone. 1990. "Political Models of the Business Cycle Should Be Revived." *Economic Inquiry* (July): 442–465.

Keynes, John Maynard. 1936. *The General Theory of Employment Interest and Money*. New York: Harcourt Brace and Company.

Michman, Ronald D. 1991. *Lifestyle Market Segmentation*. New York: Praeger.

Naisbitt, John. 1982. *Megatrends*. New York: Warner Books.

Naisbitt, John, and Patricia Aburdene. 1990. *Megatrends 2000*. New York: William Morrow.

Ohmae, Kenichi. 1982. *The Mind of the Strategist*. New York: Penguin.

Phillips, Kevin. 1991. *Politics of Rich and Poor*. New York: Harper Perennial.

Samli, A. Coskun. 1992. *Social Responsibility in Marketing*. Westport, CT: Quorum Books.

Shapiro, Isaac, and Robert Greenstein. 1991. *Selective Prosperity*. Washington, DC: Center on Budget and Policy Priorities.

Tomasco, Robert. 1990. *Downsizing: Reshaping the Corporation for the Future*. New York: American Management Association.

Weston, J. Fred, and Kwang S. Chung. 1990. "Takeovers and Corporate Restructuring: An Overview." *Business Economics* (April): 6–11.

Zarnowitz, Victor. 1990. "A Guide to What is Known About Business Cycles." *Business Economics* (July): 5–13.

2

The Key Features of Turbulence Impacting the Business Environment

INTRODUCTION

One may take one of two opposing positions regarding the impact of turbulence on the business population. First, as turbulence continues, the frail and less competent businesses will automatically fail, and the overall efficiency and effectiveness of existing business populations will be enhanced. Second, as businesses come under the fire of turbulence, those that happen to be slim and efficient cannot survive. Only those that happen to be big and fat are likely to survive. Those who survive are not necessarily efficient, but they have resources on which to survive through hard times.

This chapter presents a discussion of how turbulence is impacting U.S. businesses and what may be the outcome of this impact. Some of the short- and long-run trends in the business population are explored, and some of the far-reaching implications are discussed.

LONG-TERM BUSINESS TRENDS

By analyzing long-term business trends that prevail in the United States, it will be possible to understand the turbulence that exists in the U.S. markets. A number of business trends are considered in this chapter: business population, business failures, and change from manufacturing to services.

The Business Population

Business populations in reasonably free (although not perfectly competitive) markets reflect economic conditions, the needs of consumers, and society's preferences in goods and services. This whole situation stems from a market-driven economy. A market-driven economy, in time, determines the nature, size, and characteristics of the prevailing business population. However, despite the fact that the economy is driven by the market, particularly starting in the early 1980s, business became extremely finance-driven. This orientation reflected itself by being concerned with bottom lines up front. This meant a bottom line was guiding or forcing the firm to function within the constraints of finances from the beginning. For instance, the chief financial officer (CFO) may decide to cut down the marketing budget by 5 percent up front. This may mean 5 percent less advertising, 5 percent less sales effort, and so on. The firm, therefore, is guided by finances rather than by the market. Finances become a means to an end rather than an end itself. Businesses, instead of functioning for a bottom line, started to be driven by a bottom line.

The decade of the 1980s, thus, has seen perhaps the most spectacular activity relating to leveraged buyouts, unfriendly takeovers, or mergers and acquisitions. Financial acquisitions of other firms became a part of the overall strategy for most major firms. This was, again, managing the company by financial manipulations. The overall orientation toward managing by a bottom line (rather than for a bottom line) created a shrinkage in the market performance and effectiveness of most U.S. firms that followed this philosophy. As large firms survived by acquiring other firms that were doing well, small firms emerged and disappeared in very large numbers. The decade of the 1980s experienced the highest rate of business failures in the history of the United States including the years of great depression.

Exhibit 2-1 illustrates the average rate of business failures for the whole decade. It indicates a very large rate of business failures as well as business bankruptcies. Business failures have gone up from 17,000 in 1981 to almost 88,000 in 1991. This is more than a five-fold increase. The number of businesses that filed for bankruptcy also increased substantially. These two sets of data are not the same. Most of the failed businesses are not bankrupt; they simply discontinue. Thus, in calculating the impact of business failures, the failure and bankruptcy data may be used in an additive manner rather than using only one or the other set of data. Exhibit 2-2 illustrates percent changes. With the exception of two

Exhibit 2-1

Business Failures, Bankruptcies, and Unemployment (1981–1991)

Year	GNP (in millions $)	Business Failures	Business Bankruptcy Filed	Unemployed* (in 000s)	Unemployment Rate
1981	3,030,600	16,794	47,415	8,273	7.6
1982	3,149,000	24,908	56,423	10,678	6.7
1983	3,405,700	31,334	69,818	10,717	9.6
1984	3,772,200	52,078	62,170	8,539	7.5
1985	4,038,700	57,253	66,651	8,312	7.2
1986	4,268,600	61,616	76,281	8,237	7.0
1987	4,539,900	61,622	88,278	7,425	6.2
1988	4,900,400	57,097	68,501	6,701	5.5
1989	5,244,000	50,361	62,534	6,528	5.3
1990	5,513,800	60,508	64,688	6,874	5.5
1991	5,672,600	87,592	67,714	8,426	7.0

*Unemployment figures are for civilians.

Sources: Business Failures — U.S. Department of Commerce. 1991. *Economic Report of the President*, 394. Washington, DC: GNP Standard & Poors Statistical Service; Bankruptcy — U.S. Department of Commerce. 1991. *Statistical Abstract of the United States*, Table 884, 394. Washington, DC: GNP Standard & Poors Statistical Service; Unemployment — U.S. Department of Commerce. 1992. *Economic Report of the President*, 334 & 340. Washington, DC: GNP Standard & Poors Statistical Service.

Exhibit 2-2

Percent Changes in GNP Business Failures, Bankruptcies, and Unemployment Figures

Year	GNP	Business Failures	Unemployed	Unemployment Rate	Business Bankruptcy Filed
1981	10.93	43.03	8.33	8.57	30.09
1982	3.91	48.31	29.07	27.63	19.00
1983	8.15	25.80	0.37	-1.03	23.74
1984	10.76	66.20	-20.32	-21.88	-10.95
1985	7.06	9.94	-2.66	-4.00	7.21
1986	5.69	7.62	-0.90	-2.78	14.45
1987	6.36	0.01	-9.86	-11.43	15.73
1988	7.94	-7.34	-9.75	-11.29	-22.40
1989	7.01	-11.80	-2.58	-3.64	-8.71
1990	5.14	20.15	5.30	3.77	3.44
1991	2.88	44.76	22.58	27.27	4.68

years, 1988 and 1989, business failures increased on a yearly basis. Bankruptcies also increased throughout this period except in 1984, 1988, and 1989. Between 1984 and 1989 the unemployment picture improved somewhat. However, it got worse suddenly in 1990 and worsened again in 1991 and 1992.

Exhibits 2-3 and 2-4 illustrate correlation coefficients. GNP correlates highly with unemployment (a negative correlation indicating that as the economy grows unemployment gets lower). Business failures also show a high correlation with GNP, indicating again that as GNP grows, business failures decline, and as GNP slows down, business failures increase.

Exhibit 2-3
Matrix of Correlation Coefficients of the Data Presented in Exhibit 2-1

	GNP	BUSF	BUSB	UNEMP	UNEMPR
GNP	1.000	0.788	0.144	−0.794	−0.832
BUSF	0.788	1.000	0.373	−0.582	−0.622
BUSB	0.144	0.373	1.000	−0.247	−0.262
UNEMP	−0.794	−0.582	−0.247	1.000	0.997
UNEMPR	−0.832	−0.622	−0.262	0.997	1.000

Exhibit 2-4
Matrix of Correlation Coefficients of the Data Presented in Exhibit 2-2

	%GNP	% BUSF	% BUSB	% UNEMP	% UNEMPR
% GNP	1.000	−0.010	−0.416	−0.877	−0.884
% BUSF	−0.010	1.000	0.173	0.297	0.315
% BUSB	−0.416	0.173	1.000	0.461	0.427
% UNEMP	−0.877	0.297	0.461	1.000	0.994
% UNEMPR	−0.884	0.315	0.427	0.994	1.000

As can be seen from Exhibits 2-1 through 2-4, an economic downturn could cause thousands of businesses to fail and millions of workers to become unemployed. These exhibits also illustrate that there are too many ups and downs in these figures that may further contribute to market turbulence.

One of the major impacts of the prolonged economic cycle of the 1980s is that more small service and retail establishments entered (and of course exited) the business population. A number of factors caused this development.

First, they were easier businesses to start. They took a minimal amount of capital and were low-cost operations.

Second, many people who are trained and educated for positions in large U.S. companies could not get jobs and were forced to opt to start this type of small firm.

Third, unavailability of venture capital created a major hindrance to start small-to-medium-size technical firms with substantially more capital needs.

Fourth, people with high levels of technical training and education found high-paying jobs easily in highly technical large companies primarily engaged in research for the armed forces or related industries. Thus, small, independent, technical firms did not emerge as a part of the business population.

Fifth, the lack of capital combined with the declining supply of highly trained technical labor force contributed to the lack of an emerging technical firm group.

As the number of retail and service establishments increased, it did not quite keep up with the population in the number of establishments per thousand of population. The number of retail establishments per thousand population declined regularly, indicating that there needs to be a minimum population base or a minimum business volume for these firms to survive. Perhaps this is one of the reasons why many small firms have failed. They were too small to begin with.

Business Failures

One of the truly misunderstood phenomena in modern market economies is business failures. Perhaps the key reason for not paying much attention to business failures stems from the logic of classical economics. If the market is perfectly competitive, as Adam Smith or Alfred Marshall advocate, then the weak and inefficient firms will fail. This process will make the economy stronger and more efficient. However, the U.S. economy cannot be farther away from Adam Smith's or Alfred Marshall's perfectly competitive market (Samli, 1992). If the economy is imperfectly competitive or not at all competitive in that it is composed of oligopolies and monopolies, then there is a major question about the role of business failures. There is no reason to assume that only the weak and inefficient will go out of existence. Indeed, in our current market economy, which is not perfect competition, the firms that are run effectively and that are slim and lean can and do go out of existence when business conditions are adverse. Very large firms, even though not efficient and not run well, can survive adversities in the marketplace because of excessive resources. Thus, while in perfect competition the survival of the fittest doctrine can be advanced, in less than perfect competition this doctrine becomes survival of the fattest, indicating that the firm survives not because it is efficient and profitable but because it has large financial resources. These resources enable it to survive the adversities of recession. These businesses can live off the fat they already have.

While business failures in less-than-perfectly-competitive economies do not make a contribution to the overall economy, their cost could be extremely high. Exhibit 2-5 illustrates various cost factors of business failures. The costs can be categorized into two categories: (1) direct costs of business failures, and (2) indirect costs of business failures. Although business failures and business bankruptcies are not the same, the same type of cost analyses are applicable to business bankruptcies. In 1991 there were over 87,000 business failures and more than 67,000 business bankruptcies.

Direct Costs of Business Failures

Direct costs of business failures are related to at least four specific areas. There are costs to creditors; direct costs of the legal process; costs of lost savings; and most importantly, costs of the proprietor's time and efforts. These four costs are discussed below.

Costs to Creditors

Although there may not be as much venture capital or as many individual creditors in small businesses as there are in big businesses, in both small and big business failures, creditors lose substantial sums. There are two aspects to this loss. Creditors lose money that might at least have been used for consumption that would have improved their quality of life. But, more importantly, they might have used these monies in more profitable ventures that might have created further economic gains. Thus, the cost of failures can be rather excessive expressed in terms of lost opportunities or quality of life.

Exhibit 2-5
Direct and Indirect Costs of Business Failures

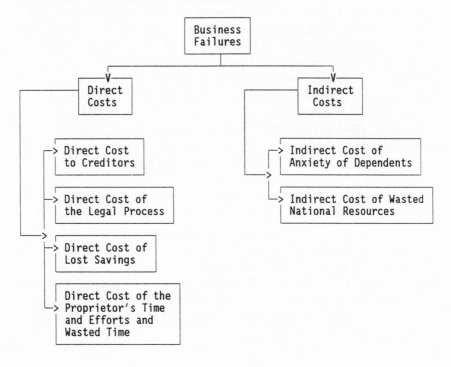

The Cost of Legal Process

Much time and effort goes into the settlement process. All this time and effort is counterproductive in that there is no new productivity and much time and effort that can be used for other productive purposes is used for unproductive activity. Assuming that in a dynamic society there are many other alternatives for productive and creative use of time and effort, the cost of the total legal process can be very high, not only to the individual but the society as well.

The Cost of Lost Savings

The resources of failed or bankrupt businesses are not used for other purposes. These resources can be large sums of money, capital equipment, and other assets. They will not only be tied up for long periods of time but also be lost in an unsystematic manner because they are used to pay off business debts. In the case of many small business failures, the lost sums are, relatively speaking, large, and they represent lifetime savings.

Time and Effort

In addition to losing their lifetime savings as businesses fail, proprietors and workers waste substantial amounts of time and energy until they find employment. Much of the time the employment they find is not in their area of specialty. Hence, their productivity is not likely to be optimized, and the society loses because of the misuse of its human resources. If there are any physical assets, they will remain idle until failure or bankruptcy procedures are completed. These procedures take a long time, and during that period valuable assets and equipment will remain unused, which is likely to be a very costly proposition for the society.

Indirect Costs of Business Failures

The anxiety of the dependents of those who lost their businesses or their jobs because of business failures is a substantial indirect cost. Not only are their lives disrupted, but also the lives of their dependents are put on hold. The dependents, instead of pursuing a career of continuing their education, may be forced to take a menial job which both in the short run and the long run might prove to be quite costly to society.

All of the direct costs discussed above have indirect cost implications at the national level. Because of the various direct impacts of business failures, national resources are wasted, which, in turn, would worsen the already adverse economic conditions. The following is a simple example.

The Disadvantage of AdVantage

AdVantage was a small advertising agency in a small Southeast university town. It employed about six people in addition to the two part-time owners, who put in substantial amounts of time and money to keep the agency going. Because of recession, AdVantage started experiencing major cash flow problems because of declining business volume and bad debts. Finally AdVantage declared bankruptcy. Company assets well exceeding $35,000 were tied up. Eventually they were sold to the highest bidder (about $5,000). The remaining equipment and fixtures stayed in a storage place in the garage of one of the owners. The employees collected unemployment for about five months as they searched for jobs. The employees' dependents (if any) also started looking for jobs. Spouses found minimum paying jobs and disrupted their college educations, or had to leave their smaller children with babysitters even though this was not their first choice. The owners lost tremendous amounts of time and at least $60,000, which significantly changed their consumption patterns and reduced their quality of life. This lost amount of resources certainly did not give a number of others (both businesses and individuals) new opportunity for advancement or new economic opportunities that would contribute to the total national economic base. If it were to be considered that this simple situation is typical, then about 65,000 business failures or business bankruptcies will indicate very large numbers of social and economic costs.

Three key points need to be reemphasized here. First, business failures primarily are a function of economic conditions (Samli, 1964). Second, business failures increase, as the economy deteriorates, and they are very costly. Third, particularly in times of recession, business failures do not represent the demise of the weak and the powerless. Thus, business cycles are very costly, and they create significant turbulence in the business sector. This turbulence, in part, expresses itself in the form of business failures. Business cycles imply significant changes in market needs, and business failures indicate a deterioration in the economic base.

CHANGE FROM MANUFACTURING TO SERVICES

John Naisbitt (1982) observed that our society is moving away from being an industrial society to being an information society. Thus, he claimed that the information explosion is changing the ways products are created. Information is particularly important because it provides change, increase in productivity, and competitive edge in the world markets. Thus, the society is becoming (or must become) a knowledge society (Drucker 1989, 1992). The critical aspects of an information (or knowledge) society is that it is putting more emphasis on generating and disseminating information than on producing products. Thus, during the late 1980s and early 1990s the U.S. society lost many high-paying manufacturing jobs and generated large groups of knowledge workers who generate and disseminate information. Along with these basic trends, the United States has witnessed the emergence of a very strong service sector. Perhaps two points are particularly critical to marketing. First, at a very high level, knowledge workers earn large sums. However, on the average, knowledge workers, particularly those who are employed in the service sector, do not earn as high wages as the workers in manufacturing used to earn. Second, knowledge workers' productivity does not go up quickly. Even if it did, it is difficult to measure. Therefore, the knowledge workers' and service workers' income do not go up fast enough.

These two employee classifications, that is, knowledge workers and service workers, whose earnings have not been as high as those of manufacturing workers, and have not been increasing fast enough, have created critical changes in income distribution. These changes are summarized by Shapiro and Greenstein (1991). Three key points are particularly critical:

1. From 1977 to 1988 the average after-tax income of the poorest one-fifth of households fell 10 percent after adjusting for inflation.
2. The middle one-fifth of households experienced an average after-tax income gain of less than 4 percent over this period.
3. By contrast, the top one-fifth of households realized an average gain in after-tax income of 34 percent. At the same time, the average after-tax income of the richest 1 percent of U.S. citizens more than doubled from 1977 to 1988, rising 122 percent after adjustment for inflation. The average after-tax income of these households reached $451,000 in 1988, up from $203,000 in 1977.

Marketing deals with people's needs, provides satisfaction for these needs, and, hence, delivers utility. These drastic changes in income have caused additional turbulence in the market place in terms of people's needs and their satisfactions.

Large groups of consumers are becoming worse off. Chances are that they will emphasize cheaper consumer non-durable goods (food, medicine, and so on) without which they cannot manage. They will deemphasize consumer durables (automobiles, appliances, homes) that are critical for the national economy's growth. By deemphasizing them, they either postpone their purchases or buy cheaper used products. Sales of used products do not generate employment and production worker income.

A very wealthy but small market is emerging. This will mean producing unique and expensive shopping and specialty goods in small quantities. This, again, will disrupt the market's continuity in its offering and production. These unique and expensive products are likely to use excessive amounts of natural resources. They will also be costly to produce because of non-existing economies of scale. These trends are likely to change the overall structure of national markets and hurt the national economy. But above all, they will create turbulence for marketing. Not only the product (and quite likely the service) mixes need to be adjusted but also prices and promotional programs need to be reevaluated. Chapters 5, 6, 7, and 8 of this book deal with these issues.

This chapter has presented some of the key reasons and implications of turbulence in the market place. In order to cope with these changes in the market, a firm has to be proactive (as opposed to inactive or reactive) in its market strategies (Samli, 1992). This means very early detection, a futuristic orientation, and a creative (and at times dramatic) development of the firm's marketing plan.

SUMMARY

Three major trends are discussed in this chapter: (1) business population, (2) business failures, and (3) change from manufacturing to services. Time and again these trends created turbulence for the business sector. Whereas one part of this turbulence is related to the shrinking economy, the other parts of it imply somewhat unpredictable change. In order to cope with the external turbulence, marketing must be proactive by being attentive to changes and perhaps moving along with them simultaneously.

REFERENCES

Drucker, Peter R. 1992. *Managing for the Future*. New York: Truman Talley Books/Dutton.

____. 1989. *The New Realities*. New York: Harper & Row.

Naisbitt, John. 1982. *Megatrends*. New York: Warner Books.

Samli, A. Coskun. 1964. "Role of Business Failures in the Economy." *University of Washington Business Review* (February): 53–63.

____. 1992. *Social Responsibility in Marketing*. Westport, CT: Quorum Books.

Shapiro, Isaac, and Robert Greenstein. 1991. *Selective Prosperity*. Washington, DC: Center on Budget and Policy Priorities.

3

Too Much Bottom-Lining and Too Little Market Orientation

INTRODUCTION

In the 1980s a new concept emerged that eventually started controlling business, government, and other organizations that have a budget for management purposes. The concept is fiscal responsibility. In essence, fiscal responsibility maintains that an individual should not spend more than what he or she makes, and the income and outgo should be equal. Of course, borrowing is critical at the individual, business, and government levels. If an individual can borrow and go to college at night, that individual is making a critical investment that will yield substantial future revenues. The same analogies can easily be developed for a business and for government. The fiscal responsibility has given way to bottom line orientation. This chapter presents a case against this kind of thinking. Instead it proposes proactive marketing to cope with environmental adversities or economic turbulence.

MARKET-DRIVEN ECONOMY AND FINANCE-DRIVEN BUSINESS

Weston and Chung (1990) state that: "deregulation in the financial services industry permitted greater freedom and flexibility, which encouraged an inflow of capital resulting in excess capacity" (7). This excess capacity, they maintain, stimulated new types of activities, some of which are very speculative. It is maintained here that this freedom followed by other tax incentives, made it extremely attractive to raid corporations. Corporate raiders have been involved in unfriendly takeovers and leveraged buyouts.

With the short-run orientation advocated by fiscal responsibility and the short-run benefits of leveraged buyouts and unfriendly takeovers, U.S. companies stopped investing in production, renovation, research, and development. Instead, they kept on buying out the competition and downsizing to make the financial profile of the company appear to be very attractive in the short run. Thus, while the economy was market driven, U.S. enterprise became finance driven. The finance-driven firm tried to influence its environment by financial manipulations (leveraged buyouts and unfriendly takeovers) and tried to adjust itself to market adversities by internal adjustment (downsizing and managing by a bottom line). While the finance-driven firm managed to survive in the short run (survival of the fattest), it not only reduced its chances of survival in the long run in the market-driven economy, it contributed to the adversity of economic conditions by discouraging investment in research and development (R&D), in development of human resources, and in infrastructure. The economy, as a whole, experienced having many more extra-large and inflexible oligopolistic firms that are much further removed from consumers and the market. In addition to not investing in research and development, in development of human resources, and in infrastructure these companies have been downsizing and not hiring.

Thus, the bottom line management combined with fiscal responsibility has helped the economy to shrink further and create further eroding market conditions.

THE COST OF LEVERAGED BUYOUTS
AND UNFRIENDLY TAKEOVERS

Leveraged buyouts increased from 11 in 1980 to 388 in 1989. In terms of value, this increase has been from $0.24 billion to $61.58 billion (Waheeduzzaman, 1992). In old-fashioned mergers and acquisitions, companies were bought out because, typically, they were not doing well and others bought them at bargain prices to run them as added activity to their overall operations. However, the frenzy of leveraged buyouts and unfriendly takeovers of the 1980s has been just the opposite. Corporate raiders of the 1980s aimed at highly productive and profitable companies. Much of the time they broke these companies into components and sold them. Thus, some of the best companies in the U.S. economy have been taken out of commission. If these companies depicted strong synergism, by breaking them corporate raiders weakened the industrial fabric of the U.S. economy. The leveraged buyout activity did not stop but accelerated throughout the decade of the 1980s (Exhibit 3-1). Although it is not shown in Exhibit 3-1, during the 1980s, divestitures also increased in very significant proportions. Although there are no specific studies indicating the relationship between these and unfriendly takeovers, it can be hypothesized that the tremendous increase in divestitures (both in numbers and volume) is an indication of the resale of some parts of the whole of those companies that were acquired through leveraged buyouts or unfriendly takeovers.

Exhibit 3-1
Leveraged Buyouts as a Part of Mergers and Acquisitions

Year	Total Mergers		Leveraged Buyouts		Leveraged Buyouts as Percent of Total	
	No. of Deals	Value ($ bil.)	No. of Deals	Value ($ bil.)	Number	Value
1980	1,558	32.8	11	0.24	0.7	0.7
1981	2,328	69.5	100	3.87	4.3	5.6
1982	2,298	60.7	164	3.45	7.1	5.7
1983	2,393	52.7	231	4.52	9.7	8.6
1984	3,175	126.1	254	18.72	8.0	14.9
1985	3,484	146.0	255	19.67	7.3	13.5
1986	4,446	205.8	337	45.16	7.6	21.5
1987	4,015	178.3	279	36.23	7.0	20.3
1988	4,000	236.4	377	46.56	9.4	19.7
1989	3,415	231.4	388	61.58	11.4	26.6

Source: Waheeduzzaman, A.N.M. 1992. "Effects of Corporate Takeovers and Leveraged Buyouts: An Extension of Strategic Models in Marketing." In *Enhancing Knowledge Development in Marketing*, edited by R. P. Leone and V. Kumar, 109–116. Chicago: American Marketing Association.

If the companies were to be purchased and kept intact for operational purposes rather than to be broken into components and resold, then companies would have purchased them for strategic reasons. Exhibit 3-2 presents such a picture. The companies are purchased in a hostile manner; however, they are purchased because strategically there is a good fit between the aggressor and the one that is purchased. This strategic fit can be in the form of production. The newly acquired company may have specific and more modern production facilities or additional production know-how that may create an additional competitive edge for the acquirer.

Exhibit 3-2
Relationships between the Acquired Firm and Acquirer

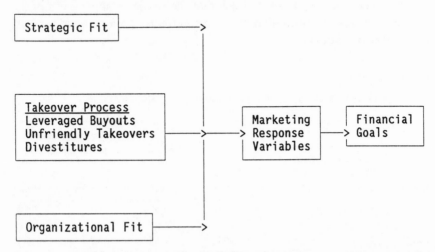

Source: Adapted and revised from Waheeduzzaman, A.N.M. 1992. "Effects of Corporate Takeovers and Leveraged Buyouts: An Extension of Strategic Models in Marketing." In *Enhancing Knowledge Development in Marketing*, edited by R. P. Leone and V. Kumar, 113. Chicago: American Marketing Association.

Similarly, strategic fit may be related to marketing. The firm that is acquired may have market niches that are exclusive. The aggressor, by acquiring the firm, can achieve easy access to these market niches.

Finally, the company that is being purchased may have certain technological features that may be used by the aggressor to improve its competitive edge. This is the third aspect of strategic fit.

The other aspect of fit between the aggressor and the company being purchased is organizational fit (Exhibit 3-2). There are at least four aspects of organizational fit.

First, the company that is being taken over may have the matching size. This may be large or small but a desirable match. In some cases the merger may create a large firm which, by sheer size, may become more competitive with other large firms in the industry. Or it may be the elimination of a large competitor in a specific market segment.

Second, the ages of the companies involved may match. While the aggressor may be a little older, the company that is being acquired could be young and may bring new blood and a brand new outlook.

Third, the company that is being taken over may have a matching similarity in leadership style. This may strengthen the newly developed organization in terms of its leadership style and implementation of an overall strategy.

Fourth, the overall organizational structure may provide a good fit. The newly acquired company may have an overall organizational fit in such a way that it may be totally downsized without losing its capability to function. Both the strategic fit and organizational fit, if used for competitive purposes, will trigger certain marketing responses (Waheeduzzaman, 1992). The enhancement in the strategy and organization would generate at least three marketing response variables.

First, it may change the market share. Particularly if the aggressor takes over a competitor that has a good proportion of the total market, the change in the firm's market share is almost automatic.

Second, there may be a change in innovation. The aggressor may enhance its competitive edge by taking over a company which has many new products or a strong research and development function.

Third, the aggressor's distribution efficiency may improve. If the company that is being acquired happens to have an efficient distribution system in the same market where the aggressor mainly functions, then the overall distribution system is likely to improve. Similarly, the company that is being acquired may be a specialist in distribution, which, again, would improve the acquirer's efficiency in distribution.

FINANCE INSPIRED TRANSACTIONS

Hise (1991) posits that from the perspective of the acquiring firm, mergers and acquisitions are consummated for a variety of reasons besides marketing strengths. However, he maintains that it is the marketing factors that often explain why mergers and acquisitions subsequently succeed or fail.

As seen in Exhibit 3-2, leveraged buyouts and unfriendly takeovers do not take place to enhance the market position or marketing capabilities of the aggressor. Rather, they take place to fulfill short-run financial goals. Whereas improved marketing capabilities would clearly provide both short-run as well as long-run profits, leveraged buyouts and unfriendly takeovers may provide great gains for the corporate raiders at the expense of those companies that are taken over as well as for the society as a whole. By taking over good, profitable, and progressive firms, corporate raiders have been and are weakening (if not destroying) the industrial fabric of the United States. As they take over competition, they are also reducing competition and creating oligopolistic firms that are far removed from the markets and consumers. They are also inflexible and uncreative (Samli, 1992). These companies are not creating new jobs, new opportunities, or new markets. Additionally, they are steadily downsizing and, hence, eliminating high-paying jobs. One last point relates to synergism. A successful company takes a long time to become synergistic in that all of its divisions work in unison and the company as a whole is more productive, valuable, and important than its components. Studies have shown that this synergy component has given a special competitive edge to Japanese industry (Hanssens & Johansson, 1991). However, because of leveraged buyouts and unfriendly takeovers many strong U.S. firms are broken into different parts and, therefore, have lost their synergistic advantages.

Thus, as large corporate raiders restructure some companies to cope with market turbulence, they are clearly and significantly contributing to the turbulence itself. One of the most critical impacts of leveraged buyouts and unfriendly takeovers is the reduction of competition.

CHANGING COMPETITION

The modern patterns of mergers and acquisitions have been in the form of leveraged buyouts and unfriendly takeovers. These patterns have limited competition and contributed to the emergence of oligopolies. Chapter 1 presented some specific information on this point. It appears that almost all major U.S. industries have taken a path toward increased oligopolies.

Oligopolies, by definition, stand for limiting competition. Even though oligopolistic firms compete among themselves, this competition in marketing terminology is primarily non-price competition (McCarthy & Perrault, 1991). Because an all-out price war is extremely costly to oligopolistic competitors, they prefer to compete in terms of service, quality, product innovation, and the like.

Although these factors of non-price competition are important, price competition is particularly critical in times of recession. If those consumers who have limited means are able to buy more products (particularly consumer durables), that would be an important growth stimulus for the economy. However, instead of being engaged in price competition, oligopolists are scaling down their operations. In 1992, GM announced the closing of some nine plants and laying off of some 70,000 workers. This scaling down activity has had a devastating impact on the already sluggish economy and has enhanced already existing turbulence. In fact, it has been concluded by Shapiro and Farrel (1990) that mergers that are not creating synergies are raising prices. From the previous discussion it may be concluded that most of the oligopolists that emerged in the 1980s are not even seeking synergism and, hence, they are contributing to higher prices (or not allowing prices to go down) in addition to restructuring the industrial complex of the U.S. economy.

One additional problem with oligopolistic companies is that they are too big and far removed from consumers. Hence, when they try to compete in terms of quality and service, they often cannot deliver.

Finally, in an oligopolistic market, entry opportunities for small newcomers are few. Oligopolists have the power and know-how to control markets, to establish their own power base, and to make it almost impossible for newcomers to enter and be successful in that market.

SUMMARY

This chapter presents a major flaw in the U.S. business system at the present time. While the U.S. economy is driven by the market, U.S. businesses are driven by finance. Thus U.S. firms, instead of adjusting themselves to market conditions, are trying to influence the market by financial manipulations. These financial manipulations have been in the form of leveraged buyouts (LBOs) and unfriendly takeovers. These activities have reduced competition and created oligopolies. Their longer lasting impact has been in blocking economic growth and progress that are the outcomes of increased rather than decreased competition.

By being extremely bottom-line oriented, major U.S. firms have downsized their organizations rather than investing in research and development, in human resource development, and in infrastructure renovation or advancement. All of these developments have contributed to the turbulence that is becoming more and more noticeable as well as more and more adverse.

REFERENCES

Hanssens, Dominique M., and Johny K. Johansson. 1991. "Rivalry as Synergy? The Japanese Automobile Companies Export Expansion." *Journal of International Business Studies* (February): 503–526.

Hise, Richard T. 1991. "Evaluating Marketing Assets in Mergers and Acquisitions." *Journal of Business Strategy* (July-August): 46–51.

McCarthy, E. Jerome, and William Perrault. 1991. *Marketing Management.* Homewood: Richard D. Irwin.

Samli, A. Coskun. 1992. *Social Responsibility in Marketing.* Westport, CT: Quorum Books.

Shapiro, Carl, and Joseph Farrel. 1990. "Horizontal Mergers." *American Economic Review* (March): 107–125.

Waheeduzzaman, A.N.M. 1992. "Effects of Corporate Takeovers and Leveraged Buyouts: An Extension of Strategic Models in Marketing." In *Enhancing Knowledge Development in Marketing*, edited by R. P. Leone and V. Kumar, 109–116. Chicago: American Marketing Association.

Weston, J. Fred, and Kwang S. Chung. 1990. "Takeovers and Corporate Restructuring: An Overview." *Business Economics* (April): 6–11.

4

The Modern Business Firm and Its Concerns

INTRODUCTION

The previous three chapters highlighted the existing turbulence in our economy with the long-term and short-term implications. It was also posited that while the economy is market driven, the modern U.S. firm has become excessively finance driven. The outcome of this extreme financial drive has taken the modern firm out of the market. Instead of interacting with the market and taking advantage of market opportunities, the modern firm is trying to take advantage of financial opportunities by buying out competition, creating oligopolies, and downsizing internally. The outcome of this behavior has been a lack of growth, a lack of research and development, and a lack of increased competitiveness. In this chapter, I discuss the concerns and constituencies of the modern enterprise. I maintain that the modern U.S. business has more responsibilities than just making money for the shareholders.

FROM STOCKHOLDERS TO STAKEHOLDERS

Businesses in the United States traditionally have been very micro oriented. All the efforts and activities of the firm have been to advance the goals of the firm. This orientation paid off quite well 150 or 200 years ago. When Adam Smith (1779) wrote his book, *The Wealth of Nations*, he specified the conditions under which perfect competition prevails. If those conditions were to prevail today and if perfect competition were to be the standard form of competition in the market place, then, having the business enterprise to function with an extreme micro orientation would be not only acceptable but also the best choice. When the conditions for perfect competition are prevalent, that is, no barriers to entry and exit, perfect information for business decision makers and consumers, perfect rationality on the part of business decision makers and consumers, and special influence on the market and in existing competition by any particular firm, then the most micro oriented firm will have to perform in the most rational manner. The field of economics can illustrate that the firms that deviate from this behavior pattern cannot survive. However, perfect competitive conditions did not exist in Adam Smith's day, and today the U.S. market is, perhaps, as far as it has been from the conditions of perfect competition. Samli (1992) has contrasted the current conditions that are prevalent in the modern U.S. market with the conditions from the time of Adam Smith. Exhibit 4-1 illustrates this contrast.

Exhibit 4-1
A Comparison of Adam Smith's Market to the Current U.S. Market

	Adam Smith's Market	*Current U.S. Market*
Enterprises	Numerous and very small	Relatively fewer and many are too big
Business decision areas	Rather simple, dealing with some basic decisions	Multitudinous, complex, and dealing with multiple decisions
Information	Limited but fully available both to business and individuals	Tremendously voluminous and not quite available to all businesses or all people
Consumers	Almost fully aware of their rather simple needs	Multiple choice options and less aware of complex needs
Entrance of enterprises	Very easy, no hindrances	In some industries it is almost impossible
Pricing power	All are price takers	Most are price makers

Source: Samli, A. Coskun. 1992. *Social Responsibility in Marketing*. Westport, CT: Quorum Books, p. 7.

The following section is taken from Samli (1992):

It has been more than two hundred years since Adam Smith (1779) articulated a freely functioning market and perfect competition. Of course, Adam Smith lived and functioned in a uniquely different environment. He saw many enterprising, very small businesses that, left alone, would function very sensibly (or rationally) to enhance their effectiveness. Entrepreneurs who ran these businesses were shrewd enough to know all that was needed for their businesses and they functioned accordingly. He also had faith in human beings who, left alone, could make simple but good decisions for their own benefit. Leaving the people and businesses alone inferred the existence of invisible hands. These are natural forces to keep the economy stable and in full-employment status.

HOW INVISIBLE ARE THE INVISIBLE HANDS?

If we consider the description of the market and conditions assumed and discussed in classical economies, it is reasonable to conclude that the market takes care of itself. If marketing does not do the job right, the invisible hand will take care of the situation by perhaps penalizing marketing or forcing it to perform in a different way. However, the unique concept of invisible hands basically implies that the market functions almost perfectly and to the utmost satisfaction of consumers. Thus, if there are irregularities or dissatisfactions related to marketing, they are expected to be taken care of.

This particular concept almost implies that not only may there be no need for social responsibility considerations for marketing, but also there may be no need for marketing.

If we compare Adam Smith's market with the current U.S. market, the picture becomes rather clear that the two have basically nothing in common and, therefore, what might have held true in Adam Smith's market is not likely to hold true in the present-day U.S. market. Exhibit 4-2 illustrates this contrast.

The exhibit compares six basic criteria relating to Adam Smith's market as well as the U.S. market: (1) enterprises, (2) business decisions, (3) consumers, (4) information, (5) entering the market, and (6) pricing power.

Enterprises

Enterprises in Adam Smith's market were very small and numerous. No one individual firm could make an impact on the market. They could freely enter or exit. They also were very competitive.

Unlike the classical conditions in today's market at the threshold of the twenty-first century, there is a tendency for oligopolies to emerge. Small businesses are not as small as those that existed in Adam Smith's times,

Exhibit 4-2

Contrasting of Perfect Competition and Current U.S. Market Conditions

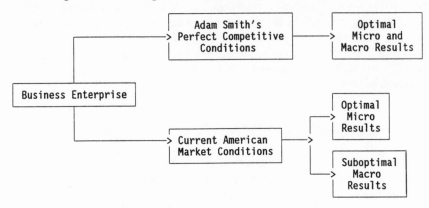

and large businesses are incredibly large. None of these existed in Adam Smith's times.

Business Decisions

In Adam Smith's time, business decisions were simple and, because of competition, not much different from certain norms that are followed by all businesses. Thus, because of simplicity and competition, businesses made what may be considered simple and rational decisions.

Business decisions in the modern U.S. market are multi-dimensional, extremely complex, and extremely numerous. It is impossible to assume that business decisions even approach rationality, let alone perfect rationality. Modern U.S. businesses have to make complex decisions and, because of the multi-dimensionality of their decision conditions, they make many decisions. Thinking that all of these decisions can be rational, leading to optimalities, is quite unrealistic.

Consumers

In Adam Smith's market consumers were aware of their needs and what they must acquire to satisfy those needs. Because of their closeness to small business units and because of the limited nature of their choice, they were able to make simple but positive decisions.

Today's consumer has a tremendous number of choices. Most of the products are complex and many of them have additives, preservatives, and other chemicals. Some of them are dangerous. Many of them have hazardous long-term effects. It is virtually impossible for the modern consumer to be rational and maximizing. Normal average consumers are typically confused and have difficulty making satisfactory decisions. Even though they may have the capability to evaluate functional product attributes in a rational manner, they lack the time and motivation to do so (Loken, Ross, & Hinkle, 1986; Engel, Blackwell, & Miniard, 1990).

Information

In Adam Smith's market information was simple and available. Neither consumers nor businesses needed access to huge data bases to make reasonable and rational decisions. Simplicity of the community and the market conditions enabled both businesses and consumers to develop access to equally simple information for their decision processes.

In the modern U.S. market, just like all the other complicated factors that are interacting with the market or influencing it, information is also complex. Information's complexity is due to two factors. First, it is extremely voluminous; an information explosion has been going on for decades. Second, many different media disseminate this information in the market place. Much of this complex information is needed by consumers as well as businesses to make decisions. Information is neither readily available nor easily accessible. This is the other end of the equation causing irrationality of consumers and businesses. These two groups cannot possibly make rational decisions when information is not readily available or easily accessible.

Entering the Market

Entry into Adam Smith's market was very easy. New businesses entered the market without any interferences. Many small businesses that were quite similar to each other managed to enter and survive in the market. Again, because of simplicity of the market and proximity to consumers, these little businesses managed to serve the market well and survive.

The modern U.S. market is not only very complex but also not quite open for entry. Today's market has many barriers to entry. Some of these are economic and others are legal. Economic barriers are related to unevenness of economic power distribution. In a number of major industries the market can be described as oligopolistic. In such cases the oligopolists are so powerful and the entry requirements, in terms of capital, know-how, and other similar resources are so outrageous, that new firms can hardly enter the market. In other industries, such as some of the consumer services, entry is rather easy, but survival is extremely difficult.

Legal barriers are related to local or federal regulations. In many industries, such as banking, insurance, or health-related activities, there are vigorously enforced strict local and federal regulations restricting entry.

Pricing Power

Pricing power of enterprises in Adam Smith's time were such that firms were perfectly competitive. With such a competitive picture comes the status of being a price taker. The price taker means that nobody has certain monopoly power to manipulate prices. All participants follow a market-determined pricing policy. However, in modern times many businesses have taken the position of being price makers. As monopolists, or at least as monopolistic competitors, they assume the role of being price makers. They have more independence and a lot more power than their counterparts in Adam Smith's time.

As seen in Exhibit 4-1 and the accompanying discussion, the invisible hands of Adam Smith's classical economic theory are no longer in existence. Because the conditions are not present for the micro economic activities leading to a macro economic optimality, it is unrealistic to expect the presence of perfect competition in the contemporary U.S. market.

THE RESULTS OF THE ABSENT INVISIBLE HANDS

The perfect competition and its implications in Adam Smith's time would lead one to believe that, unchecked, the market conditions are so appropriate that the economy takes care of itself and the people who are participating in it. This would mean that the economic well-being of the consumer and the society are both taken care of and approaching certain optimality.

If these conditions are prevalent and these outcomes are acknowledged, then there is no reason for social responsibility considerations. The firms that do not act responsibly will be boycotted by consumers and will be eliminated. Thus, the firm's dutiful and accountable behavior is related to its economic performance, and the market takes care of the efficient and effective as it eliminates the inefficient and ineffective.

However, as we establish that the conditions that prevailed in Adam Smith's market leading to perfect competition are no longer present, we must discard the invisible hands. Invisible hands in Adam Smith's time were construed to be certain natural forces that invariably adjusted the market conditions for the better. They eliminated the inefficient, or provided better utilization of resources, or created more competition if there were extraordinary profits in an industry.

In today's market we can still assume that there may be some semblance of invisible hands. But, if they do function, there is no reason to assume that they will function in a positive manner. Because of the lack of information and unevenness of economic power, invisible hands may cause further accumulation of economic power or misallocation of resources, among other malfunctions.

The reason for malfunctions in the present market is that the necessary conditions for perfect competition are not present like they might have been in Adam Smith's market. Thus, there is no reason to assume that both at the micro and macro levels economic and marketing functions will lead to satisfactory results and that the market, if uninterrupted, will take care of everything. The lack of perfect competition and Adam Smith's invisible hands, by definition, implies the possibility of the presence of many malfunctions in the market and the economy. These malfunctions or less-than-optimal results are furthered by irresponsible behavior on the part of businesses. Part of the irresponsible behavior causing less than optimalities — in fact, unsatisfactory economic results — is related to marketing. Social responsibility in marketing, therefore, would be — indeed, should be — geared toward achieving those results that would have been achieved if competition were perfect and the invisible hands were truly functional. Without certain socially responsible behavior by the overall marketing process in the society, there is no possibility of optimizing the economic performance of the society and providing optimum quality of life for the society.

It has been said that the corporate entity's first responsibility is to its stockholders. If the company makes good decisions and shows a healthy existence, its shareholders benefit. Simultaneously, the firm's contribution to the society and the economy also becomes optimal because the assumptions of perfect competition automatically make this condition a reality. However, unlike in Adam Smith's time, if the company is completely micro oriented it is not automatic that its overall economic contribution is optimized also.

Exhibit 4-2 illustrates this situation. Conditions that are conducive to less than perfect competition would lead to less than optimal macro economic results. In terms of the economy as a whole, this situation implies the existence of the performance results discussed in Chapter 3. The firm, in generating less than optimal conditions, may be laying off people (downsizing), cutting down its research and development activity, and not putting enough effort into renovating productive facilities or furthering the development of its human resources.

Here is one illustration of this situation. While this book was being written, the mass media were discussing a situation that Time-Warner Company has experienced. The company announced that it was laying off about 500 key people, which admittedly would weaken the company's competitive capabilities and overall performance. However, the chief executive officer of the company received (according to estimates) $79 million. With a reduced salary paid to the chief executive officer the company could have paid $100,000 to each person rather than firing each one. This is a single case. If such behavior were to prevail in most major companies of the United States, the economy would likely shrink by alarming proportions.

As the corporate entity gets away from macro optimization, it becomes extremely critical to consider its broader reach and responsibilities. It becomes extremely important for the corporate entity to expand its considerations from the well-being of stockholders only to include stakeholders. In fact, it is argued here that the stakeholder orientation is quite likely to be more beneficial to the firm from a macro perspective. Trying to satisfy the needs of larger groups and contributing to the economic pool of society by supporting stakeholders will, in the long run, expand the firm's own market opportunities and reduce undesirable economic volatility.

THE STAKEHOLDERS

The economic impact of the modern corporate entity is far reaching. Not only the administrators, workers, and stockholders but also the corporation's immediate customers, unattached consumers, and the society as a whole are part of this far-reaching economic power. Ideally it is the same corporate entity that provides growth, innovation, and stability, in short, overall opportunity for the individuals and, therefore, for the society as a whole.

However, the first three chapters of this book illustrated that the modern corporate entity is not fulfilling these expectations for the society. Traditionally U.S. enterprises have had three key goals — continuity, growth, and prosperity. Let us analyze the current status of these goals.

Continuity

Management and other business books have always made a distinction that, while individuals have a limited life span, the corporate entity may have an indefinite life. Of course, many companies exist today that have been serving three or four generations of customers. Companies such as Sears, Ford, GE and numerous others are almost traditional Americana. However, in the 1980s many companies started grooming themselves for corporate raiders rather than for continuity. These companies wanted to be bought out by their competition. Similarly, on the other end of the spectrum, corporate raiders, for over a decade, kept on scouting for other companies to prey on. When companies have this type of short-run pre-occupation, they are not likely to put time, effort, and financial resources into long-term growth, research and development, and investment in infrastructure and human resources. Thus, many companies during this era, instead of putting their resources into continuity, emphasized financial manipulations as well as buying out and selling each other. This behavior has had a clearly negative effect on the economy. Part of this impact is discussed in the first three chapters of this book; however, the key point that needs to be emphasized is that much of the U.S. economic growth and development, until the 1980s, was because of the corporate objective of maintaining continuity. Without such an orientation, a corporation's contribution to the society's well-being not only diminished but also, in some cases, was reversed.

Growth

The U.S. economy, since its inception, has been growth oriented. Not only administrations, civic groups, and individuals have been pro-growth but also, particularly, the corporate entity has always been prone to growth.

Growth up until the 1980s meant expanding productive capabilities and market opportunities and making sure that this growth would yield better returns on investment. However, since the 1980s, growth has become financial manipulation. Leveraged buyouts and unfriendly takeovers have created large oligopolistic firms that reduced competition and reinforced the newly emerged "culture of contentment" (Galbraith, 1992).

Galbraith (1992) maintains that those who enjoy their economic, social, and political condition attribute social virtue and political durability on the basis of their own status. They are not likely to change. They are likely to be for the status quo although there is much evidence against it.

In Galbraith's words:

The beliefs of the fortunate are brought to serve the cause of continuing contentment, and the economic and political ideas of the time are similarly accommodating. There is an eager political market for that which pleases and reassures. Those who would serve this market and reap the resulting reward in money and applause are reliably available (1992, 2).

If the contentment culture is real, then it provides reinforcement for the discussion that the U.S. corporate entity in the 1980s was not proactive. It did not want to grow in the traditional way; hence, it did not provide growth in employment, in income, or in infrastructure. Thus, those who were content tried to maintain the status quo. This orientation enhanced the conditions that are providing turbulence in the U.S. market system. Businesses that did not pursue strategies and plans to maintain continuity and growth have contributed to the less than impressive performance of U.S. economy in the 1980s and early 1990s.

Prosperity

Traditionally, U.S. firms sought out profits that would yield prosperity to shareholders, owners, and capitalists. This prosperity always has been pursued by efficiency, good management, effective competition, and overall good performance.

When the corporate entity started having an orientation different from continuity and growth, then the prosperity that it generated became selective. While a few rich became very rich, the society in general lost. The poor became poorer, and many middle class consumers became poor. Furthermore, unlike the traditional ways of generating growth and wealth, this selective prosperity came about not by generation of wealth but by redistribution of wealth from those who have limited means to those who already are rich.

It may be concluded that the business firm plays an extremely important role in the well-being of the U.S. market. If the firm deviates from its traditional orientation of pursuing continuity, growth, and prosperity as depicted in Exhibit 4-3, the firm can make a negative contribution to the economy by initiating economic stagnation or a downfall trend. However, while this is happening, there may also be economic redistribution of income and wealth from those with limited means to those with almost unlimited means. One illustration of the latter is financing leveraged buyouts with junk bonds. This financial scheme caused much grief and anguish among middle class retirees and young, ambitious people who thought they made a good investment for the future. They all lost their investments. Despite the jail sentences and other legal actions, the architects of these manipulations have come out richer and quite well off at the expense of thousands.

Exhibit 4-3
The Traditional View of the Role of Business in the Economy

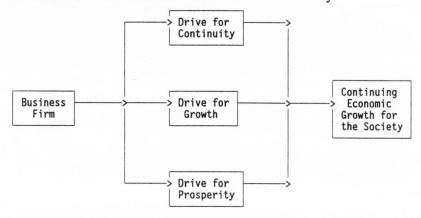

SUMMARY

This chapter makes a critical statement. The overall responsibility of the business entity has moved from considering the well-being of stockholders to considering the well-being of stakeholders. Economic impact of the U.S. enterprise has become far reaching. However, unlike the traditional orientation, U.S. corporate entities in the 1980s and early 1990s have not pursued continuity, growth, and prosperity. Instead, they sought out a short-run bottom-line at any price. This overall orientation disrupted economic growth and a healthy balance in the market place; in fact, it contributed to a downfall spiral and a questionable redistribution of income and wealth. It not only caused the current turbulence in the U.S. economic scene but also furthered that turbulence by worsening the adverse economic conditions through the process of searching a maximum bottom-line in a shortest possible time.

REFERENCES

Engel, James, Roger D. Blackwell, and Paul W. Miniard. 1990. *Consumer Behavior*. New York: CBS College Publishing.

Galbraith, John Kenneth. 1992. *Culture of Contentment*. Boston: Houghton Mifflin.

Loken, Barbara, Ivan Ross, and Ronald L. Hinkle. 1986. "Consumer Confusion of Origin and Brand Similarity Perceptions." *Journal of Public Policy and Marketing* 5: 195–211.

Samli, A. Coskun. 1992. *Social Responsibility in Marketing*. Westport, CT: Quorum Books.

Smith, Adam. 1779. *The Wealth of Nations*. London: George Routledge.

5

Early Diagnosis of Marketing Problems to Facilitate Proactive Marketing Action

INTRODUCTION

It has been suggested in the previous four chapters that environmental turbulence has become intensified. As the turbulence is felt by the firms in the economy there are two schools of thought. Lusch and Laczniak (1989) have suggested that the turbulent environment will increase the competitive intensity of an industry. Among larger firms, this higher level of competitive intensity is hypothesized to result in increased use of non-price marketing strategies. Of course, large firms also opted to buy out competition and downsize. Typically, oligopolistic firms engage in non-price competition. Therefore, this point of view is almost a given. The second school of thought relates to small entrepreneurial firms. Davis, Morris, and Allen (1991) posit that, as the environment becomes more uncertain or turbulence accelerates, firms react by implementing more marketing activities and become more market oriented. They further maintain that "a turbulent environment suggests that a firm must be willing to be more innovative, more proactive, and generally take more risks than in relatively stable environment" (49).

Thus, there is an indication that in both cases marketing functions change under increased turbulence. It appears that the large firms approach the problem differently than small firms. In this chapter a discussion is presented in favor of being more proactive as displayed by entrepreneurships (or small businesses). The first step of proactivity is to develop a system of early diagnosis of marketing problems stemming from turbulence. This chapter dwells upon becoming more proactive based on early diagnosis.

EARLY DIAGNOSIS OF MARKETING PROBLEMS

Consider the following:

The manager of X restaurant usually comes to work and finds a line of people waiting for his establishment to open. One morning, as he comes to work, he realizes that there is no longer a line waiting to go to X restaurant.

The manager of the retail establishment Y usually sees customers come in, browse around, and, typically, buy a number of things. Lately, of the people who come in and browse, only a very few are buying something in the store.

The Z bank recently realized that many of its elderly customers (who happen to be a majority of its customers) have been leaving the bank without giving any reason.

These are a few examples of early indicators. Samli and Barker (1984) pointed out that perhaps one of the most important strengths that can be attributed to marketing in a corporation is its ability to generate symptomatic information. They go on to say that before the financial statements indicate if the firm is in good or bad shape, which is too late for corrective action, marketing research can generate a lot of information that would indicate the positive status or show a symptom of pathological conditions. By doing so the firm can identify its problems, undertake corrective action, and even (or perhaps more preferably) develop new and proactive marketing strategies that will enable it to survive, grow, and prosper. Thus, symptomatology is part of the marketing feedback mechanism. It is likely to reveal symptoms of pathology or indications of positive impact relative to the firm's marketing performance (Milroy, 1965). Although knowing that the firm's performance has been positive is important, it is not quite as vital as detecting symptoms that may indicate deep and serious problems. By identifying symptoms, the firm can identify the problems it is facing and their pathological causes (Abell, 1978; Samli & Barker, 1984).

A MODEL OF MARKETING SYMPTOMATOLOGY

Marketing management can be analyzed on the basis of an input-output model (Alderson, 1965; Kotler, 1991). This model is presented in

Exhibit 5-1. A large variety of marketing inputs are utilized in the firm's marketing policies and strategies. Among these are the firm's reputation, know-how, salesforce, products, brands, patents, and the like. As the strategies are implemented by further use of these marketing inputs, marketing output emerges. This output takes the form of products, services, distribution, and so on. The end result of marketing output is the firm's overall marketing impact. This impact expresses itself in many ways. Among these are the firm's profits, consumer's attitude toward the firm and its products, and the firm's market share.

As seen in Exhibit 5-1, the firm's marketing impact is determined by feedback composed of indicators and symptoms. Detecting the negative impact through symptoms enhances the awareness of a total mechanism of chain reactions. Some years ago Audi 5000 went through some difficulties. When a number of consumers reported that the car did not stop or went backward when it was supposed to go forward, the company did not pursue this as an engineering problem. The president of Audi North America appeared on national television and accused those people of not knowing how to drive. The reaction of the market was negative. It put the progress of Audi in the U.S. market on hold. The company did not increase sales or gain a larger share of the market. The early indication of user problems should have created a chain reaction of engineering corrections combined with an effective advertising campaign (Hulbert & Norman, 1977).

The necessary chain reaction as a result of the detected indicators and symptoms is illustrated in Exhibit 5-2. Monitoring the market

Exhibit 5-1

An Input/Output Model of Strategic Symptomatology

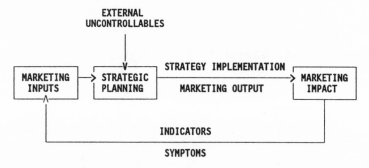

Source: Samli, A. Coskun, and Tansu Barker. 1984. "Early Diagnosis of Marketing Problems." *Management Forum* (March): 22–26.

performance of the firm is bound to yield early symptoms of the impact in the market place. Consider, for instance, a newly introduced auto model that in two months has amassed three times the repair bills of any newly introduced car in the past, in its particular category. If this symptom does not generate a chain reaction very quickly, the company stands to lose large sums of money. Similarly, a newly developed videocassette recorder may have four times the return rate that any videocassette recorder had in the past. The purchasers have been returning the equipment before the trial period is over and have registered their dissatisfaction. Once again, if this symptom is not quickly detected and corrective action not forthcoming, the firm will have a very costly experience in the market place.

Just what are some of the key symptoms? Although there are no complete lists, there are some basic symptoms. However, it must be posited very strongly that the firm can have its own unique symptoms that are early and decisive. This indicates the alertness of the marketing group of the firm (Makridakis & Wheelwright, 1978).

MARKETING SYMPTOMATOLOGY: A CLASSIFICATION

Particularly in turbulent times, the symptoms indicating that the firm may be in serious trouble need to be observed very closely. These symptoms can be classified into three categories. The first is the marketing output — the actual performance record of the management. By following this performance record, it is possible to detect certain symptoms of problems that are in the making.

The second category is inputs. By analyzing the key marketing inputs, certain problems can be uncovered. Perhaps, even prior to output

Exhibit 5-2
The Chain Reaction in Strategic Symptomatology

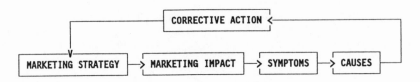

Source: Samli, A. Coskun, and Tansu Barker. 1984. "Early Diagnosis of Marketing Problems." *Management Forum* (March): 22–26.

symptoms, the input symptoms may indicate potential problems. A new product, for instance, at a pretest stage may indicate that it may be hazardous to health. Or company A's product may not compare favorably with that of company B. Similarly a panel or consumer focus group response is not quite favorable to the company's newly proposed advertising campaign. These and many other early symptoms based on marketing inputs can eliminate major problems that may be in the making. These problems can be prevented very early by acting on these early indicators.

The third category, unlike the first two sets of symptoms, is composed of more specific indicators dealing with inputs and outputs, occurring either one at a time or simultaneously. If, for instance, the firm detects that its promotional messages are not congruent but rather are contradictory. Thus, the promotional messages sent out by the firm are offsetting each other and the firm is not making any progress in the market place. These three groups of symptoms are discussed in the following sections.

Output Symptoms

As seen in Exhibit 5-3, six output symptoms are distinguished in this chapter.

Market Position

Market position of the firm is a good indicator of the firm's marketing effectiveness. The companies that are capable of determining their market position periodically are often in a unique position to detect their own well-being. Market position, well in advance of the profit and loss statement, would indicate if the overall performance of the firm is satisfactory or deteriorating.

Exhibit 5-4 illustrates the outcome of the market position assessment process. As seen in the exhibit, the assessment, in this case, is based on two dimensions — quality and value. Exhibit 5-4 indicates that our firm is doing very well in the market. However, this illustration presents only one point in time. It is possible that the picture would not be as positive if the analysis were to take place in a different time. It is possible that our firm's position has deteriorated, and competitor A is beginning to look like a major threat. In times of turbulence, special attention may be paid to the practices of competitor A to see if it is not using a better anti-recession marketing strategy than our company. For instance, as recession sets in, competitor A steps up its advertising selectively and starts emphasizing

Exhibit 5-3
Some Key Strategic Symptoms

General Marketing Symptoms (Output)
1. Market position
2. Sales volume
3. Repeat sales
4. Product-market match
5. Corporate image changes
6. Market share

General Marketing Symptoms (Input)
1. Specific policies versus economic conditions
   A. Decreasing activity in recession
   B. Increasing prices in inflation
   C. Doing both in stagflation
2. Wrong marketing goals
3. Wrong positioning
4. Downsizing, rightsizing, or wrongsizing

Specific Symptoms (both Input and Output)
1. Incongruent promotional messages
2. Marginal revenue of promotion less than marginal cost
3. Increase in customer complaints
4. Abnormal proportions in brand switching
5. Increased unit pricing causing volume decline
6. Product mix changing in the wrong direction

Source: Samli, A. Coskun, and Tansu Barker. 1984. "Early Diagnosis of Marketing Problems." *Management Forum* (March): 24.

different lines of products that are more attractive in times of economic hardship.

Sales Volume

Again, long before the financial statements of the company appear, detailed analysis of sales volume indicates if the overall performance is in the right direction. More specific analysis of sales volume in terms of sales territories, sales force, and product group sales performance can more specifically indicate the strengths and weaknesses of the firm within given economic conditions. It must be realized that these strengths and weaknesses may change as the nature or the intensity of the turbulence in the market place changes.

For instance, as the recession deepens, it may become obvious to our company that our product groups A, B, and C may be selling better than

Exhibit 5-4
Market Position Assessment

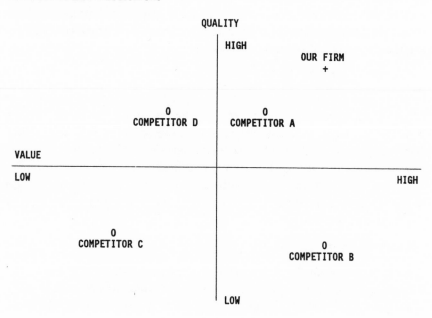

products D, E, and F in markets X, Y, and Z. If it is expected that the recession will continue and deepen, it will be wise for the company to produce more A, B, and C group products and emphasize its sales efforts even more on markets X, Y, and Z.

Repeat Sales

If the company's sales are increasing but only a very small proportion of the total is repeat sales, malaise would be indicated. Perhaps, although they may be extremely appealing at the outset, the firm's products may have some basic defect or design deficiency. The buyers do not remain happy with them, and, therefore, they do not come back for repeat purchases.

Product Market Match

If the product market matches that have been very successful are deteriorating because of some basic changes in our markets due to changing market conditions or intensifying turbulence, the chances are that there will be serious problems in the near future. To the extent that product market match becomes a product market mismatch, the company is in grave danger. While a good product market match is quite profitable, a product market mismatch becomes very unprofitable. Perhaps all matches, in time, can become mismatches; however, a proactive firm must detect the tendency of some matches to become mismatches quickly, and must take corrective action immediately.

Corporate Image Changes

When, many years ago, DuPont managed to successfully switch its image from "producers of death" to "better things for better living through chemistry," the company gained more acceptance by the market and was getting healthier. This acceptance and health improvement would pay in terms of profits, longevity, and competitive edge. Similarly, however, the image could be deteriorating, and the company may not be in the position to detect this. This deterioration could eventually lead to the demise of the firm.

Market Share

Since market share is one of the most important indicators of the firm's marketing impact, early detection of market share changes can be very important. If the firm's market share is becoming negative and one competitor distinctly is gaining that market share, it is possible to determine what our company is or is not doing vis-à-vis the competition. This type of analysis would help the firm to get back on course from its derailed position.

Input Symptoms

Four special input symptoms are identified in Exhibit 5-3. It must be reiterated that there are many more input symptoms. Individual businesses must be aware of their own specific symptoms.

Specific Policies versus Economic Conditions

Input symptoms are clearly the beginning of more proactive marketing programs. As economic conditions change, performance of the firm changes as well. However, a corporate slow-down based on economic recession should be separated from an internal problem causing a decline in sales. A firm that is totally inactive will not only not know the difference but also not do anything about the situation. A reactive firm can move against the corporate sales' slow-down, but it may be too little, too late, and particularly ineffective. Only a proactive firm will immediately determine if the slow-down is because of internal or external factors and will make significant changes in its inputs toward capitalism in the changing economic conditions or improving the firm's performance by changing its strategic posture through changing marketing inputs.

Three key external economic problems that are related to the conditions of the economy and function as input symptoms are identified. These are recession, inflation, and stagflation.

Recessions are a critical form of economic turbulence. Understanding that a business slow-down is due to externally uncontrollable recessionary factors would enable a proactive firm to take counter recessionary measures fast.

Inflation, if continued and intensified, would have a significant impact on the firm's performance. Proactive firms can develop anti-inflationary practices. Such practices could improve their market position and their profit picture.

Stagflation is perhaps the worst of all possible worlds (Samli, 1989). In 1978 and again in 1982, stagflation has shown its face and its dangerous nature. In both cases, significant economic slow-down was combined with significant inflation. Stagflation factors, again, if detected early and counteracted proactively, can be nullified and perhaps turned into a profitable pasture for a firm.

If the firm cannot read the symptoms properly, it endangers its own survival. For example, firing the sales manager in the middle of an acute recession, rather than accelerating the sales and promotional efforts, is likely to backfire and threaten the survival of the firm.

Wrong Marketing Goals

As market conditions change, the basic corporate goals may become inappropriate. Changing competitive conditions and the nature of the domestic economy caused A&P, the largest grocery chain in the United States, to experience significant annual losses. The chain had an unrealistic goal of being number one at any cost. Similarly, during the past decade and a half, Sears, Roebuck & Company has diversified into major financial areas and lost its focus in retailing and consumer satisfaction. As a result, the company has been facing critical financial hardship. These and other similar experiences must stimulate proactive behavior in terms of reevaluating corporate goals swiftly if the firm wants to survive and prosper.

Wrong Positioning

Either originally or because of subsequent changes in the market, a firm that positioned itself erroneously is bound to lose. Positioning itself as an outstanding researcher and a futuristic company, a major pharmaceutical firm that came up with a controversial and borderline dangerous drug, might be particularly hurt because it positioned itself wrong and unrealistically built up expectations of the market toward its services. Such a firm may be in the right market for the wrong reason or in the wrong market for the right reason. But in either case it cannot last very long if it does not rectify its mismatched target markets and its marketing efforts.

Downsizing

In recent years the concept of downsizing has emerged. Corporate entities, in order to reduce bureaucracy, eliminate various managerial layers and improve the profit picture, more often referred to as the bottom line. In turbulent times, during which the markets are undergoing significant changes, organizational restructuring is not prudent and is basically dangerous. If the firm is not rearranging its manpower resources to counteract the turbulence, it is likely to find itself in even greater danger after the downsizing activity. Although some companies refer to downsizing as rightsizing, it is maintained here that in turbulent times it is clearly wrongsizing. As discussed in Chapters 2 and 3, in addition to enhancing the firm's vulnerability, downsizing also contributes to economic turbulence.

Specific Symptoms

There are certain specific symptoms that are more specific than input or output symptoms. These symptoms do not constitute as serious an illness as any of the first two groups of symptoms. However, their presence implies substantial losses for the company that eventually could jeopardize the firm's viability. Similarly, early detection of these specific symptoms, if followed by proactive marketing measures, can help the firm to survive successfully through turbulent times. Some of these specific symptoms are listed in Exhibit 5-3.

Incongruent Promotional Messages

The firm's promotional activity may either be unsuitable or may have become unsuitable for its target market. Furthermore, the messages may be contradictory and, therefore, may be offsetting each other. The bank that is trying to communicate with the upper middle class but succeeding to communicate with the lower middle class, for instance, is likely to become more and more ineffective as it continues to operate in the same manner. Furthermore, it may begin to lose money. The bank is sending mixed messages and, therefore, not succeeding in developing a clear-cut image; it is in jeopardy. By the time it realizes that there is a problem, it may be too late.

Marginal Revenue of Promotion Is Smaller than Marginal Cost

In any case, if the firm cannot approximate whether its advertising or other promotional efforts are paying off, then the firm is in a difficult situation. Although advertising and other promotional activities are extremely important, if the firm is not pursuing an effective overall promotional policy, its losses will be more than just the cost of promotional activity. The firm will become less and less effective in communicating and therefore satisfying its target markets.

Increase in Customer Complaints

All things being the same, if the firm's customers are complaining more often than before about some specific aspects of the firm's business, there appears to be a serious problem in the making. Some of the customers of the firm will complain very early. Their opinions can be used to identify the problem more succinctly and determine remedial measures. The firm needs to develop the type of sensitivity to these early indicators that will lead to the initiation of proactive solutions.

Abnormal Proportion in Brand Switching

A certain amount of brand switching goes on constantly. However, if the firm's research indicates that large numbers of its customers are switching to competing brands, there is strong reason to be concerned. This excessive switching activity may be because of a deficiency in the firm's marketing activities. The firm may not be making any changes while its competition is showing a higher level of proactivity by taking advantage of major changes in the economy.

Increased Unit Pricing Causing Volume Decline

Many firms use unit costing as a basis for their pricing decisions. However, if in a recessionary period the sales volume goes down, the unit cost-oriented accounting system may indicate that the costs are going up and the prices must follow suit. When costs go up because of the lost economies of scale, it is necessary to hold the price line or even lower it in order to regain the lost economies of scale. Otherwise, increased prices because of the increased unit cost will lead to further decline in the sales volume.

Product Mix Is Changing in the Wrong Direction

Just as in the case of the U.S. auto industry in the 1980s, while the economic, social, and political conditions all pointed in the direction of small and efficient U.S. cars, the industry insisted on having its traditional large cars, with few exceptions. As a result, the industry lost more than 25 percent of its market to small foreign imports. Thus, if a company's product mix goes against the trends, as happened to the U.S. auto industry, the company is bound to experience large losses.

SUMMARY

When the turbulence in the market place becomes more acute, which has been discussed in the first four chapters of this book, early diagnosis of marketing problems becomes a necessity. This chapter puts forth Samli and Barker's (1984) concept of "strategic symptomatology." Strategic symptomatology maintains that marketing inputs of the firm eventually create marketing impact. This impact early on puts out some symptoms of positive or negative happenings in the market place. Early identification of these symptoms would lead to swift and effective corrective action.

Three groups of symptoms are identified in this chapter. These are input symptoms, output symptoms, and specific symptoms. A number of symptoms are discussed in each group. Perhaps the most important point in this chapter is that the firm can develop its own unique indicators that would enable it to develop proactive marketing plans to take advantage of economic turbulence that, otherwise, would be simply devastating.

APPENDIX: OPPORTUNITY BUDGETING

A strong case is made in this chapter and throughout this book that a proactive marketing orientation is necessary for the firm to counteract the turbulence that is experienced in the market place. Such a proactive marketing orientation implies being able to change rather fast but, even more importantly, being able to take advantage of new opportunities that may emerge in the market place as the economic conditions change. Such activity requires a major commitment on the part of the firm so that provision can be made for changing and newly emerging market opportunities. This commitment calls for organized, continuous, and disciplined efforts on the part of the firm to commit some of its resources to actual and potential results as the changing and emerging opportunities are used to best advantage. Drucker (1980), in conjunction with this type of thinking, proposed a new concept. He called it an opportunity budget.

In his words, "One way to exercise assignment control and to concentrate is to have two budgets, an operational budget for the things that are already being done and an opportunities budget for the proposed new and different ventures" (Drucker, 1980: 42). He goes on to say that, "for the opportunities budget the first question is: 'Is this the right opportunity for us?' And if the answer is 'Yes,' one asks: 'What is the optimum efforts and resources this opportunity can absorb and put to productive use?'" (42). Finally, he says that "the opportunities budget should be optimized, i.e., funded to give the highest rate of return for efforts and expenditures" (42).

Thus, the opportunity budget is a proactive budget that is based on the most suitable and promising market opportunities that the firm is experiencing. Obviously the most important point in the development of opportunity budget is the identification and prioritization of the changing and newly emerging opportunities. A process to accomplish this goal is presented in this section.

Zeroing in on the Opportunities

Exhibit A5-1 illustrates a five-stage development leading to successful construction of an opportunity budget. The stages are specified from very general external to most specific internal.

The first stage is establishing opportunities. Measuring markets, their growth rate, and their need changes can be extremely important opportunities. It is important to assess these and convert them into products or services and approximate sales volume.

Once the opportunities are established, they need to be scaled down on the basis of the threats. Threats stem primarily from increased competition or deteriorating market conditions.

The next step is to analyze the firm's own capabilities. Its strengths must be such that it could take advantage of the external market

Exhibit A5-1
Zeroing in on the Opportunities

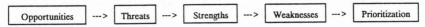

opportunities. This means translating market opportunities into the firm's resources and capabilities.

The strengths of the firm need to be scaled down against its weaknesses. Even though the new market opportunities may be especially attractive, if capitalizing on these implies not eliminating the firm's weaknesses and not using its strengths then it is quite likely that those opportunities may not have a high priority in the firm's marketing plans.

Finally, the fifth step is prioritization. Once a number of opportunities are isolated and scaled down, some of them are likely to be most attractive. It is extremely important to prioritize opportunities from most to least attractive (Kotler, 1991).

Developing the Opportunity Budget

The effectiveness of the opportunity budget, first and foremost, depends on the firm's capability of prioritizing its opportunities. If the first phase of the prices, that is, zeroing in on the opportunities, is not done adequately, the results could be detrimental

As stated by Drucker (1980), opportunity budget should be optimized. This means while the funding for different opportunities should be maximized, there should also be ample resources allocated to unforeseen opportunities as well as drastic changes in the prioritization or the ranking of these opportunities. Thus, the whole process needs to be flexible enough to optimize the firm's efforts to counteract turbulence and capitalize on opportunities.

REFERENCES

Abell, D. F. 1978. "Strategic Windows." *Journal of Marketing* (July): 21–26.

Alderson, W. 1965. *Dynamic Marketing Behaviors.* Homewood, IL: Richard D. Irwin.

Davis, Duane, Micheal Morris, and Jeff Allen. 1991. "Perceived Environmental Turbulence and Its Effect on Selected Entrepreneurship, Marketing and Organizational Characteristics in Industrial Firms." *Journal of the Academy of Marketing Science* (Winter): 43–50.

Drucker, Peter F. 1980. *Managing in Turbulent Times.* New York: Harper & Row.

Hulbert, J. M., and E. T. Norman. 1977. "A Strategic Framework for Marketing Control." *Journal of Marketing* (April): 12–20.

Kotler, P. 1991. *Marketing Management.* Englewood Cliffs, NJ: Prentice-Hall.

Lusch, Robert F., and Gene R. Laczniak. 1989. "Macroenvironmental Forces, Marketing Strategy and Business Performance: A Future Research Approach." *Journal of the Academy of Marketing Science* (Fall): 283–294.

Makridakis, S., and S. C. Wheelwright. 1978. *Forecasting.* New York: Wiley.

Milroy, N. 1965. "The Disintegration of an Information System." In *Management*

Control Systems, edited by Antony et al., 17–29. Homewood, IL: Richard D. Irwin.

Samli, A. Coskun. 1989. *Retail Marketing Strategies*. Westport, CT: Quorum Books.

Samli, A. Coskun, and Tansu Barker. 1984. "Early Diagnosis of Marketing Problems." *Management Forum* (March): 22–26.

6

Product Decisions in Turbulent Markets

INTRODUCTION

Product decisions are very critical in economic turbulence. Proactive marketing practices must concentrate on product decisions that are flexible, futuristic, and creative so that changing conditions of the market can be converted into corporate profits as well as economic expansion. As turbulence sets in, consumers alter their attitudes toward buying and consuming products. Similarly, a growing concentration of economic power is observed. Manufacturers' brands (or national brands) in such economic times lose ground in favor of private brands. Competition at the small scale retail level increases (Summers, 1987). This chapter distinguishes the need for more flexible product portfolios. In this effort a new concept of futuristic product portfolios is introduced. Both in current as well as in futuristic product portfolios, there should be products that are suited for economic decline periods as well as products that are more suited for economic boom periods. It is maintained here that the firm's product mix is a powerful tool to cope with turbulence in a proactive manner.

DECLINE IN U.S. PRODUCT DEVELOPMENT

U.S. competitiveness, both on domestic and international fronts, has been declining since the late 1970s. This is, at least partially, because of the prevailing extreme short-run orientation in U.S. industry. Such an orientation is reflecting itself in terms of having a void in the area of developing products that are groomed for the future. Although such futuristic products are risky, they are also very profitable (Samli, Palda, & Barker, 1987). New innovations, futuristic products, and breakthroughs take time to get established; however, if the products are developed and accepted, then payoffs are rather spectacular. Most major corporations, such as IBM, Xerox, and GE, have had such experiences. However, because of the widespread long-term entanglement among U.S. companies, only a handful with vision are working on developing products that are likely to be successful in the future. A number of reasons have been cited for U.S. firms' not being prolific in developing new products. Some of the reasons revolve around top management's failure to accelerate the development of new products based on new technologies (Gupta & Wileman, 1990). Others maintain that engineering design has been neglected, which is causing the drought in new product innovation (Dixon & Duffey, 1990). Still others claim that there is a general lack of interest in new product development (Spencer, 1990).

The failure to innovate for domestic as well as international markets is evident in many companies (*Business Week*, November 24, 1986). Almost all of these explanations have an underlying trend that is an excessive short-term orientation in overall management philosophy. This behavior stems primarily from undue emphasis on bottom line and on managing by it rather than for it. This behavior, coupled with financial manipulations in the form of leveraged buyouts and unfriendly takeovers (see Chapters 2, 3, and 4), has caused far less than adequate funds to be made available for research and development. This situation is making it extremely difficult for companies to achieve breakthroughs, increase their product mixes, and sharpen their competitive edge.

INNOVATION AND MARKET OPPORTUNITIES

Innovation is risky but profitable. Exhibit 6-1 illustrates four separate scenarios that a firm is likely to encounter (Samli et al., 1987).

Scenario One: Business opportunities often revolve around a market for an existing product. This was the case when Burger King entered the market that was dominated by McDonald's and when Pepsi Cola challenged Coca-Cola. The products are very similar, so the entry is through imitation, complementing the existing product (for example, barriers for a

Exhibit 6-1
Product-Market Opportunities

Scenario	Product Development Function	Time Frame	Risk Factor
Scenario 1 (M+P+) Market is ready, recognizable and there are numerous products in existence to satisfy this need.	Imitative designs either complementary or substituting for existing products.	Very short run	Low risk activity. Short-run positive ROIs*
Scenario 2 (M+P−) Although there are clear-cut needs, there are no readily available products.	Modifying design either by expanding product line or deviating from it along with some innovation.	Short run	Intermediate risk activity. Short-run to intermediate-run good ROIs.
Scenario 3 (M−P+) Through existing research and development and technology new products are being developed. However, there is no obvious market for these products.	Innovative designs either taking existing inventions and developing new products or simultaneously creating new products as by-products of others developed.	Intermediate to long run	High risk activity. Possibly numerous ROIs; however, a few will be very high.
Scenario 4 (M−P−) Ongoing basic research may one day lead to development of new markets.	Basic research emphasis leading to major breakthroughs and inventions.	Very long run	Very high risk activity. Great ROIs if product is developed and accepted.

*ROI = return on investment

Source: Adapted and modified from Samli, A. Coskun, Kristian Palda, and A. Tansu Barker. 1987. "Toward a Mature Marketing Concept." *Sloan Management Review* (Winter): 45–52.

car), or substituting a new, better product (for example, a color television for a black-and-white one) (Alderson, 1957). The orientation is short-run in the sense that product use can be learned very quickly. Because people in general are familiar with McDonald's, they may accept or reject Burger King quickly. Thus, the level of risk for the introducer, which is low, is mainly because of competitive activities. The emphasis is not solely on the product but rather on elements of marketing mix. If the product is suited to people's needs and is marketed aggressively and effectively, it will get accepted. Although there may not be large profits, it is easy to show a positive return on investment quickly.

Scenario Two: This is a typical short-run challenge in the most familiar sense of the marketing concept. It involves a potential market whose characteristics are deduced from communications with the potential buyers. Consumer research indicates that certain unsatisfied needs create a market for a new product. The new product development process is undertaken: idea generation, screening, concept specification, development testing, and commercialization. Typically, the product's design results from deviation from existing products. The degree of innovation is rather minimal. As seen in Exhibit 6-1, the market is already present and the product is not too difficult to adjust to market needs. Although higher than in Scenario One, the absolute level of risk here is still not very high. If successful, in this situation marketing would provide a high return on investment in the short run. Development and marketing of concentrated frozen orange juice and of skim milk are examples of this scenario.

Scenario Three: Basic research by a company itself or by other non-profit organizations may lead to product ideas for which the market is not well identified or still undeveloped. These new product concepts may develop as the result of directed research and innovative activity or as by-products of other research. Because this scenario is usually based on years of research and development, it is very expensive. Developing a product in a vacuum involves high risk. Many products developed in this manner are not likely to be successful. However, some of those that will be accepted by the market will bring very high returns on investments. The chip in the electronics industry, minicomputers, and camcorders were all created directly as a result of major research projects. Similarly, other products such as Corfam and Tang were by-products of other research explorations.

Scenario Four: In the 1950s and 1960s, U.S. firms spent large sums of money on basic research, hoping to generate breakthroughs. Basic research often does not yield specific commercial results — but it can.

Today, high technology research, particularly in the areas of genetics and biology, is leading to significant new products and services. Basic research, by definition, is not related directly to existing markets. Thus, the probability of generating products that will create breakthroughs is low; however, a society makes progress particularly by these break-throughs. It is difficult today to imagine conducting business without copiers, computers, faxes, and many other products that were basically breakthroughs.

Scenarios One and Two are more consumer-oriented and rarely result in innovation. They conform to what Bennett and Cooper (1981) call the "market pull" of new product development. Scenarios Three and Four require substantial investment in research and development. They are "technology pushed." Studies show that high-growth firms concentrate more on technology push, while slow growth companies emphasize market pull (Romano, 1990). However, most new products today are imitative or deviative and, hence, are not in Scenarios Three and Four (Samli et al., 1987).

While companies in recent years are concentrating more and more on managing by a bottom line, they are not emphasizing technology push but are being satisfied by imitative and deviative product development activ-ity. This type of activity is more short-run oriented than high technology based, research oriented, or substantive in terms of stimulating the economy and facilitating breakthroughs. Companies, for their own benefit and also for the society's benefit, must put more emphasis on technology push product developments than what they have been doing recently.

However, this is a high-risk, very costly proposition. It is necessary to facilitate this type of activity by finding ways to reduce risk and encourage such activity in the form of developing futuristic portfolios.

Perhaps consumers are unable to articulate new ideas that will result in product breakthroughs. Because of excessive dependence on consumer feedback, marketing has not been extremely successful in developing futuristic products that are basically more technology pushed than demand pulled.

If the proposed product is quite futuristic, high tech, and unusual consumers have some difficulty in evaluating the concept or the product. Typically, consumers' perceptions are limited to their own experience. Their ability to sort out and articulate their needs is circumscribed; and their opinions about an unfamiliar product are subject to change. If we believe that consumers buy products consistent with their self-image and group norms, then it is natural that many new products, especially those involving high technology, will be rejected by the average consumer (Samli et al., 1987). Furthermore, the consumer may not have the education or the perception to articulate his needs or desires. Even though some consumers are able to provide information about conscious desires and needs, as they articulate their needs clearly, it is virtually impossible to extract information about their equally important unconscious needs. Thus, depending totally on consumers' awareness of their needs as the basis of new product or new product concept evaluation leads away from any genuine innovation in product development.

EVALUATING FUTURISTIC PRODUCT IDEAS

It is clear from our discussion that purely consumer-evaluated new product concepts may be handicapped in the sense that the further away they are from the consumers' realm of reality, the less chance they have for approval. Thus, because of traditional evaluation processes, the more futuristic and far-out the proposed product, the less chance it has to become a reality.

In order to remedy this situation, Samli et al. (1987) have proposed a different procedure. Exhibit 6-2 presents this particular model.

The overall pattern of this procedure is not dramatically different from other similar treatments that are found in different textbooks. However, Exhibit 6-2 displays a number of unique propositions.

The first step — idea generation — can come from within the corporation or from government, university, or jointly sponsored research efforts among others. Somebody must be doing basic, solid research and development in order for truly innovative product concepts to emerge.

Internal feasibility assessment, the second step, can use various techniques. This is the major phase where many of the ideas are eliminated because of a lack of feasibility. Most of the time, those ideas that call for a smaller basic investment or are more suitable for the existing facilities and characteristics of the firm are likely to be judged more feasible than others. Because product development teams today are so present-oriented, most future-oriented ideas are put on the back burner at this stage.

Third, concept testing and specification of the features of the proposed new futuristic product need to be achieved by future-focused groups made up of future-oriented and sophisticated people. We envisage a group of scientists, corporate executives, specially selected consumers

Exhibit 6-2
Development and Evaluation of Futuristic Products

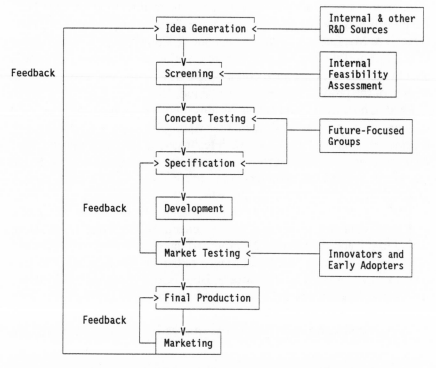

Source: Adapted and modified from Samli, A. Coskun, Kristian Palda, and A. Tansu Barker. 1987. "Toward a Mature Marketing Concept." *Sloan Management Review* (Winter): 45–53.

(for example, literary critics, consumer advocates, business professors), and innovators who are open to futuristic product ideas.

Market testing, too, must be accomplished using unusual consumers. They should be innovators and early adopters, since more ordinary consumers have difficulty relating to breakthrough products. Consumer innovators, as reported in a number of studies, are from higher income groups. They are well educated, highly exposed to mass media, socially active, opinion leaders, cosmopolitan, and venturesome (Samli et al., 1987). Along with experts and heavy users of related products, they can effectively evaluate technology pushed product ideas. Although there are some practical differences in finding and grouping these consumers, the diffusion theory literature has focused noticeably on their characteristics (Gatignon & Robertson, 1985).

If it is possible to develop such future-focused groups, they will be able to assess the success possibilities of futuristic products. Although such groups are difficult to organize, a number of techniques have been developed and are being tested for future-focused and innovator panels (Danko & MacLachlan, 1983; Dickerson & Gentry, 1983). They appear to be most useful when a realistic representation of the product is made. It should include not only an accurate visual description but also a detailed outline of the product's potential use (Wind, 1982).

Finally, not only should specially constituted consumer groups be used for concept testing as well as market testing but also nonconventional techniques should be used. One such technique is Hedonic analysis. This analysis probes multisensory fantasy and emotive aspects related to the use of proposed new products. It is particularly useful when testing products that are innovative or futuristic.

Similarly, research indicates that it is possible to use market transaction data to estimate the demand for product characteristics. Such information would imply acceptability of the proposed innovative product. Of course, these data need to be applied broadly rather than myopically, so that consumer preferences would surface. Both Hedonic analysis and market transaction data can be used in a straightforward manner to the application of well-tested econometric techniques (Samli et al., 1987).

Thus, companies must develop innovative, new and futuristic products.

FUTURISTIC PORTFOLIOS

Developing products that may not be satisfying existing needs but will satisfy needs of the future can make a significant contribution toward improving the quality of life in the future. Futuristic portfolios create major and minor breakthroughs for future company growth in revenues and profit (Samli & Zabriskie, 1992).

The key in the overall process is being long-term oriented. However, all futuristic products may not have the same degree of capability to fight off economic turbulence. Thus, instead of one or two, a healthy number of products may be included in the futuristic product portfolio of the firm.

Just how do we develop futuristic product portfolios? The answer lies in a three-stage process. Exhibit 6-3 illustrates these three phases. They are: (1) developing a process for generating futuristic product ideas, (2) evaluating product ideas for economic worth and feasibility, and (3) prioritizing the ideas for the futuristic portfolio.

Exhibit 6-3

A Process for Developing a Futuristic Product Portfolio

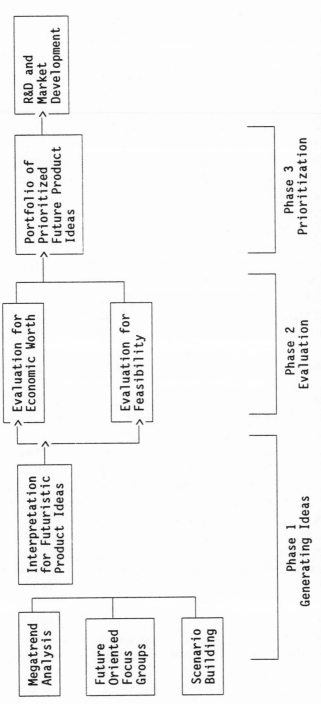

Source: Adapted from Samli, A. Coskun, and Noel B. Zabriskie. 1992. "Developing Futuristic Product Portfolios: A Research Construct for Long Range Success." Working paper, University of North Florida.

Generating Futuristic Product Ideas*

Most current new product development systems are somewhat against futuristic products. These systems are heavily dependent on consumer or buyer feedback, which in turn is dependent on the limited perception and experiences of the consumers or buyers. Too often these consumers or buyers are unable to articulate their needs or wants in terms of a futuristic perspective. Latent needs and desires that may identify futuristic product possibilities are rarely identified by most survey research methods currently in use. It is a special type of consumer that can articulate these possibilities, and special research efforts are needed to find these people and draw out their ideas.

It is suggested that there are at least three methodologies that can be used. The first of these is the use of futuristic focus groups or panels consisting of special people. Both of these would be composed of consumers who have been screened and identified as being innovators or early adopters in the product area. In addition to evaluating futuristic product ideas, these groups can participate in a process to generate new product ideas. Another approach to generating futuristic product ideas is related to the study of societal megatrends. In the 1980s there were a number of attempts to identify major U.S. trends that transform the lives of consumers and their consumption patterns. Among such attempts are those by Ohmae (1983), Naisbitt (1982), and Drucker (1980). Naisbitt's first megatrend, for example, is from an industrial to an information society. This megatrend implies a fast transfer of information to control manufacturing processes. It would lead to a futuristic idea of having robotics or using expert systems in production sequences. Use of computer-controlled cutting in textile sweatshops is an example that is related to this megatrend. Those in many manufacturing areas can easily foresee numerous futuristic products that are related to the production process, yet are driven primarily by information that results in higher consistency, reliability, and quality of output. Similarly, all key trends in our society have futuristic product implications.

A third methodology available for generating futuristic product ideas is one that corporations began to use in the 1970s and 1980s in connection with their strategic planning — building scenarios of the future (Linneman & Klein, 1985). Scenario building is a technique of long-range forecasting that attempts to foresee future changes in an industry. By first monitoring the environment to identify existing or emerging

---

*This section is co-authored by A. Coskun Samli and Noel B. Zabriskie.

external changes, the significant strategic issues are identified. These issues are then analyzed to create a scenario of what the business climate will be in the industry three, five, or more years ahead. Usually more than one scenario is developed, depending on the assumptions made about the speed, timing, and impact of the identified changes (Schnaars, 1987).

Once the scenarios are created, the one that management thinks will not likely occur is selected. From this scenario are deduced the ways in which current markets may change and the new market opportunities that may emerge. It is from these changes and new markets that potential futuristic product ideas may emerge. In fact, some corporations use scenario analysis and the market opportunities or threats to go beyond finding futuristic product ideas as a basis for building long-range corporate strategy (Leemhuis, 1985).

There are at least two differences between the megatrend and scenario-building methodologies. First, scenarios are usually much more focused on changes in an industry. That is, environmental monitoring searches for changes in trends relevant to an industry, while megatrend research focuses on the implications of a broad trend in society. Second, scenarios are developed by company planners, while megatrends are often identified by people outside the company who may be perceived as being authorities or gurus in the industry or in the product area. Thus, in some cases, these two techniques can be complementary rather than mutually exclusive.

Evaluating Futuristic Product Ideas

Once new product ideas are generated, a two-part evaluation process will be needed to identify the best ones for further development. The first part determines the economic worth of the proposed futuristic product and the second part evaluates the feasibility of these products within company capabilities. There are a number of evaluative techniques used as the preliminary evaluation method for determining economic worth of an idea (Samli & Zabriskie, 1992). These techniques basically attempt to approximate the present values of a product (or an investment) or some measure of accumulated net benefits at some future point in time. These future benefits or present values are all related to estimated acceptance of the product in the market place and some estimate of future sales volumes.

After evaluating futuristic product ideas for economic worth, the ideas need to be evaluated in terms of identifying their feasibility regarding the company's needs and capabilities. This evaluation will help to identify the level of risk that the product ideas present. The feasibility analysis should include a minimum of four areas: expertise of company personnel, manufacturing abilities, financial requirements for development, and compatibility with company marketing and distribution systems. There are many detailed sets of factors to be considered when performing a feasibility analysis. Similarly, there are numerous techniques that can be used for this purpose (Hayes & Garvin, 1983).

Prioritizing the Futuristic Portfolio of Products

Given a number of generated futuristic product ideas, and the evaluative techniques to be used, it is reasonable to assume that the ideas will fall into different categories within the futuristic portfolio. It is suggested that the portfolio have the same categories as the Boston Consulting Group classification of stars, cash cows, question marks, and dogs, although other categories could also be used. Based on whether the product is a futuristic star or a futuristic cash cow, companies must make critical decisions regarding the utilization of their resources for present versus future uses. This area is not quite adequately researched and needs particular attenuation to assure the future of the company as well as U.S. industry.

PRESENT VERSUS FUTURE

Although quite a bit of emphasis has been put into the futuristic product development as a way of hedging against unexpected future turbulence, it must be reiterated that the future is tomorrow's present. That is, the firm must have products at its disposal ready to be launched.

Marketing experts justifiably recommend investing in new products during an economic downturn (*Wall Street Journal*, October 28, 1992). New product development presents an opportunity to get ahead of rivals who are not making similar investments. However, the same position could be taken for an unexpected economic boom or excessive inflation based on extended prosperity. Companies need to have products appropriate for these unexpected turbulent times.

However, at the writing of this book, the United States is in a deep and wide recession. In 1978, when the country underwent stagflation (a combination of inflation and economic stagnation), a research study stated that consumers described the economic impact in the following manner:

Prices will be a lot higher in the future.
It is harder to make ends meet.
I am more careful with my money.
It is harder to make financial plans.
I am less happy than I used to be.
I must buy less of everything.
I must delay purchases of durable goods.
As a consumer I have changed my habits and preferences.
As a consumer I am more frustrated than I used to be (Shama, 1980, 95).

Marketing can receive many valuable hints and make some significant product policy decisions by evaluating the responses to this particular study.

Similar product decision activity is reported by the *Wall Street Journal* (October 28, 1992). In 1992, introductions of health, beauty, household, and pet products were up in comparison to 1991. Particularly in the non-food categories, manufacturers were trying to get the most money out of brand names. The cheapest way to do that is to take a big brand name and stretch it. Procter and Gamble, for instance, introduced a liquid Comet bathroom cleaner, extending its mainstay Comet scouring powder line. Gillette was extremely aggressive in 1992 by promoting Sensor razors. Riser Company of Ohio, which owns 50 supermarkets and an ice-cream manufacturing plant, instead of cutting back, poured money into building new stores, fixing up existing ones, and providing new services for shoppers.

Not only manufacturers, but also retailers and service companies must consider adjusting their product mix and service mix.

Serkissian (1989) points out five major trends:

1. Retailers who focus their product line closest to their customers will be strong.
2. Specialists in major categories such as Toys R Us will continue to grow.
3. Everyday low pricing is here to stay.
4. Catalog and direct mail will continue to divert dollars away from traditional retailers.
5. Information technology will provide a special competitive edge. MIS and point-of-purchase systems will allow retailers to maintain the most appropriate merchandise mixes.

Throughout this chapter it has been maintained that a comprehensive understanding of customer needs, both at present and in the future, contributes significantly to the success of new products. However, because of turbulence, companies must always be ready to launch new products and be proactive to counteract the negative impact of turbulence.

Exhibit 6-4 illustrates this overall orientation. Overall orientation emphasizes the need for new product development in the present as well as in the future. This orientation is described as proactive. The firm must aggressively counteract economic turbulence before the turbulence causes the firm's demise. The key concept in the exhibit appears to be a self-contradictory thought. However, proactive counteraction implies that, based on early indicators, the company takes a proactive position and develops products that would counteract turbulence and take advantage of the changes in the market place.

Exhibit 6-4

Counterturbulence Product Policies

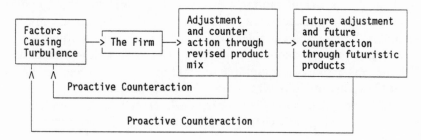

SUMMARY

This chapter makes a very important point by emphasizing proactive product policy decisions on the part of the firm in order to counteract turbulence. First, the opportunities created by the product and market relationships are explored. It is maintained here that the firm must accelerate technology pushed product development because it is very effective in terms of maintaining a competitive edge as well as being very profitable. In developing such products, future focus groups are considered very useful.

In developing futuristic product ideas, three different techniques are discussed: future-focused groups or panels, megatrend analysis, and scenario building. Once the ideas are developed, futuristic product portfolios need to be constructed. This construction takes three phases: (1) generating ideas, (2) evaluation, and (3) prioritization.

Finally it is reemphasized that counteracting the turbulence in a proactive manner implies adjusting products and product mixes both in the short run as well as in the long run. The firm should always be in the process of developing new products to protect itself as well as to maintain its competitive edge.

REFERENCES

Alderson, Wroe. 1957. *Marketing Management and Executive Action.* Homewood, IL: Richard D. Irwin.

Bennett, R. C., and R. G. Cooper. 1981. "The Misuse of Marketing: An American Tragedy." *Business Horizons* (November-December): 51–61.

Danko, W. D., and J. M. MacLachlan. 1983. "Research to Accelerate the Diffusion of a New Renovation." *Journal of Advertising Research* (June-July): 39–43.

Dickerson, M. D., and J. W. Gentry. 1983. "Characteristics of Adopters and Non-Adopters of Home Computers." *Journal of Consumer Research* 10: 225–235.

Dixon, John R., and Michael R. Duffey. 1990. "The Neglect of Engineering Design." *California Management Review* (Winter): 10–23.

Dougherty, Deborah. 1990. "Understanding New Markets for New Products." *Strategic Management Journal* 11: 59–78.

Drucker, Peter F. 1980. *Managing in Turbulent Times.* New York: Harper & Row.

Gatignon, H., and T. S. Robertson. 1985. "A Propositional Inventory for New Diffusion Research." *Journal of Consumer Research* 11: 849–867.

Gupta, Ashok K., and David L. Wileman. 1990. "Accelerating the Development of Technology-Based New Products." *California Management Review* (Winter: 24–44.

Leemhuis, J. P. 1985. "Using Scenarios to Develop Strategies." *Long Range Planning* 18(2): 30–37.

Linneman, Robert E., and Harold E. Klein. 1985. "Using Scenarios in Strategic Decision Making." *Business Horizons* (January-February): 64–74.

"More Than Ever, It's Management for the Short Term." 1986. *Business Week* (November 24): 92–93.

Naisbitt, John. 1982. *Megatrends.* New York: Warner.

Ohmae, Kenichi. 1983. *The Mind of the Strategist.* New York: Penguin.

Romano, Claudio A. 1990. "Identifying Factors Which Influence Product Innovation: A Case Study Approach." *Journal of Management Studies* (January): 75–95.

Samli, A. Coskun, Kristian Palada, and A. Tansu Barker. 1987. "Toward a Mature Marketing Concept." *Sloan Management Review* (Winter): 45–53.

Samli, A. Coskun, and Noel B. Zabriskie. 1992. "Developing Futuristic Product Portfolios: A Research Construct for Long Range Success." Working paper, University of North Florida.

Schnaars, Steven P. 1987. "How to Develop and Use Scenarios." *Long Range Planning* 20(1): 105–113.

Serkissian, Richard V. 1989. "Retail Trends in the 1990s." *Journal of Accountancy* (December): 44–55.

Shama, Auraham. 1980. *Marketing in a Slow-Growth Economy.* New York: Praeger.

Spencer, William J. 1990. "Research to Product: A Major U.S. Challenge." *California Management Review* (Winter): 45–53.

Summers, Andrew. 1987. "Strategic Food Marketing in a Turbulent Environment." *Food Marketing* 3: 28–33.

"To Outpace Rivals, More Firms Step Up Spending on New-Product Development." 1992. *Wall Street Journal* (October 28): B1, B13.

Wind, Y. 1982. *Product Policy*. Reading, MA: Addison-Wesley.

7

Pricing Decisions in Volatile Markets

INTRODUCTION

Pricing is possibly a company's most important decision, also a source of internal conflict. Marketers with their sights set clearly on the market place think that they know what the price should be. However, finance people, who are primarily concentrating on costs, have different views. Knowing how to assemble a clear pricing strategy, how to maximize the potential of discounts, and when and how to increase prices all are extremely critical skills that marketers must display (Winkler, 1990).

According to Norwood W. Pope (1989), the turbulence that occurred in the U.S. economy has ended for some businesses such as banking, but, for others, it is continuing at full steam. Pope maintains that with the emergence of interstate banking came strong resources, sophisticated marketing techniques, and a fearless attitude toward expansion. Technology played a significant role in banking, particularly in the areas of data retrieval and storage elements for marketing use. Deregulation forced banks and some other industries to address liability pricing issues. Market segmentation, niche marketing, and market positioning became increasingly important (Pope, 1989; Kotler, 1991). However, the turbulence, in general terms, is not over. In fact it is quite possible that there will be an indefinite continuation of turbulence. Thus, businesses will have to learn how to market effectively in volatile markets. This chapter points out the importance of pricing decisions in volatile markets and the complexity of making proactive pricing decisions.

PRICING: A RELATIVELY UNSOPHISTICATED MARKETING TOOL

As market turbulence becomes more pronounced, marketing decisions and decision making processes need to be more sophisticated so that proactive marketing policies can be successfully put in place.

Classical pricing decisions, typically, are not proactive in that they do not have the flexibility and fine tuning capable of responding not only to the changing economy but also to changing target markets and newly emerging market segments. Instead, traditional pricing practices have taken two clearly identified routes: demand-oriented pricing and cost-oriented pricing.

Demand-Oriented Pricing

All marketing and micro economics books deal with this basic orientation. It describes price as the point at which a buyer and seller agree to exchange goods and services in the market place (Lancioni, 1991). The typical practice in this basic pricing orientation determines total demand and establishes an optimum pricing point on the basis of the firm's cost function and the estimated demand function. Economics books indicate the optimum pricing point to be the maximum position where marginal cost is equal to marginal revenue (Kotler, 1991; Samli, 1989). Exhibit 7-1 illustrates a classical demand-oriented pricing that will maximize the profit picture if the demand is measured accurately and the product or the service in question is priced right. The theories of marginal cost and marginal revenue are in a typical marketing or micro economics book. These theories will not be discussed here. Instead, we will discuss why this is not the most adequate pricing approach.

There always have been many market segments, and each segment, typically, has different demands and different values that may be interpreted as price. The classical supply and demand analysis leaves portions of the market and, hence, much potential revenue out of the equation. Exhibit 7-2 illustrates the maximum market price chosen that is based on supply and demand analytics. The areas above and below the maximum market price are all revenue areas that do not materialize as actual revenues for the firm. This is because of one maximum price for the given market. Obviously some consumers will pay more and others less for that product or service. The proportion of those who would pay more or less will vary as market turbulence changes. Thus, by using

Exhibit 7-1
Demand and Supply Analytics

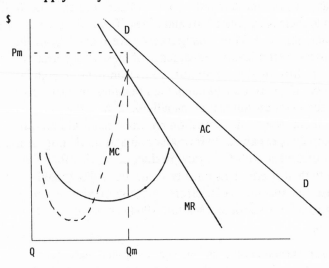

Exhibit 7-2
Market Price and Total Revenue

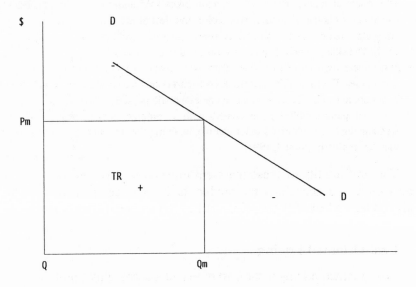

traditional pricing approach the firm is constantly losing revenues that do not materialize.

Today, customers demand goods and services that are individually tailored to their particular needs and tastes. Typically, customers get these goods and services. Thus, the markets have moved from mass production to mass customization. Emergence of mass customization is basically a violent shift in the competitive environment. It enhances market turbulence. If the executives cannot tell that their industry is undergoing a shift to the mass-customization paradigm, then market turbulence intensifies for them. Mass customization requires major alterations in the way that companies organize their production and marketing. It implies providing customers with the exact product or service they desire, tailored exactly to their needs. This must be achieved without making the customers sense the special skills, effort, and complexity required to provide these goods and services (Maital, 1991). Consider, for instance, the following:

A customer enters a music store and chooses several music selections from some 5,000 individual songs. A sales clerk punches in the buyer's choices. In a few moments, out pops a customized cassette.

Create-A-Book, a special service provided by a children's book company, uses PCs and laser printers to personalize Children's books, printing by request one's own child's name as the central character throughout the book.

The National Bicycle Industrial Company in Japan offers 11,231,862 variations of its 18 models of racing, road and mountain bikes sold under the Panasonic brand. Customer's choice of model, size, color and design are faxed to the factory. A computer creates custom blueprints, robots measure, weld and paint the frame to order. The skilled workers put on the final and finer touches.

Watch buyers own more than one. They wear them as color coordinated fashion accessories. Based on this premise, ETA Switzerland created so many models that a buyer could be almost certain that no one else could possibly wear the same watch.

A paint company supplies paint dealers with a computer that measures the light frequencies of a customer's color sample, enabling the dealers to mix a paint that matches perfectly (Maital, 1991).

The profitability of these mass-customization activities depends not only on how successfully the product or the service is customized but also on how adequately the price charged reflects the buyers' values.

Cost-Oriented Pricing

Cost-oriented pricing is the cost of manufacturing plus a profit margin. Perhaps, because of its simplicity, this pricing process is the most commonly used. It is simple, almost automatic, and leads to similar prices among firms with similar cost structures (Cannon & Morgan, 1990). Basically, the technique has four major faults: (1) considers only cost, (2) does not consider competitors' price competition, (3) does not consider market conditions, and (4) creates circular reasoning.

First, cost-oriented pricing, more commonly known as cost plus pricing, considers only cost. Most cost functions are U-shaped, indicating that, up to a point of production, if the number of units produced increases cost per unit goes down. As Exhibit 7-3 illustrates, fixed cost per unit varies as the number of units produced increases. Similarly, variable cost per unit remains the same as the number of units produced increases. In the exhibit, assume at the point T_1 the quantity demanded by the market is DT_1. At this point, with a given mark up per unit produced, the price is PT_1. Assume that during a recession the quantity demanded by the market shrinks to DT_2. The cost of producing this amount is significantly higher because of the losses in economies of scale. The new price in this case becomes PT_2, which is significantly higher than the previous price of PT_1. Thus, cost plus pricing, used as described, is likely to create inflation in addition to already existing recession.

Second, cost plus pricing does not consider competitors and price competition. It simply and very myopically considers the firm's own internal considerations.

Exhibit 7-3
Cost Per Unit and Price Changes

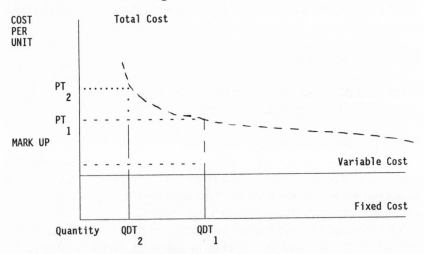

Third, cost plus pricing does not consider market conditions. As seen in the above example, when the firm needs to reduce its price, it ends up raising it as the recession gets deeper.

Fourth, cost plus pricing creates circular reasoning. Because the quantity demanded is low, the revenues are low, and because the revenues are low, the firm increases prices. The increased price further reduces the quantity demanded and the vicious cycle starts all over again. Thus, cost plus pricing, even though easy and practical, is unrealistic and dangerous. The company using this approach is likely depriving itself of the advantages of market opportunity. Similarly, cost plus pricing can reduce the firm's competitive edge by disabling it from responding to changing market and competition.

Cost plus pricing, by ignoring market and competition, does not make use of price and competition elasticity concepts. These concepts are critical, particularly in recessions, booms, and other turbulent times.

PRICE ELASTICITY AND MARKET TURBULENCE

Price elasticity, although discussed in marketing literature, is rarely practiced by the practitioner and rarely advocated by marketing academics as an important pricing tool because it is too complex and too difficult to compute (Samli, 1989).

As a concept, price elasticity implies the consumer's reaction to price changes. It may be defined as the change in quantity demanded that is attributable to a 1 percent change in price. If the quantity demanded exceeds 1 percent, demand is considered to be elastic, but if it is smaller than 1 percent, demand is considered to be price inelastic. It is calculated as:

$$\%\Delta Q / \%\Delta P$$

where $\%\Delta Q$ = percent change in quantity demanded
          $\%\Delta P$ = percent change in price.

Any standard economic text presents a fair treatment of this concept. From a marketing perspective, elasticity is important as an indicator of a store's, a product's, a brand's, or a company's competitive advantage or monopolistic power. Inelasticity in demand regarding price means monopoly power and elasticity implies a lack thereof.

If the demand that a company commands is such that price increases yield a less than proportionate decline in quantities, then it is implied that the demand is inelastic and that the store has a substantial degree of monopoly power. In such cases, the firm does not have to be engaged in price competition. Rather, it may be more readily engaged in non-price competition, emphasizing other variables of the marketing mix (Samli, 1989). In such a case, there is also some implication that the company can hold the price lines while the competition is reducing prices. Similarly the company may be able to raise prices somewhat while the competition is holding the price lines.

In times of recession, the former situation may be particularly functional. The firm, because of the elasticity function that it is facing, if it were to lower the price, is not likely to have extra revenue. Therefore, holding price lines while others are lowering their prices may be a more reasonable approach. The firm may do much better by trying to sell more at the same price than trying to raise its prices.

It is rather dangerous for a firm to experiment with price increases or decreases without measuring demand elasticity. Because it is quite difficult to measure demand elasticity exactly, perhaps a better approach is to approximate the demand elasticity by using a series of factors, including (1) competition, (2) importance of the product, (3) urgency of need, (4) ease of want satisfaction, (5) impact of total prices, and (6) economic conditions (Lynn, 1967).

APPROXIMATING PRICE ELASTICITY

The six factors used to approximate demand elasticity are:

1. Competition. Competition implies the availability of close substitutes or, in general, the company, the product, or the store have some critical competitors that are quite similar to the company, the product, or the store. In such cases, it can be deduced that customers could easily go to competitors. This situation makes demand elastic in that if the price were to be raised, more than a proportionate number of customers would go to competitors. Thus $\%\Delta Q / \%\Delta P = >1$.

2. Importance of products. If the company's products are important to customers or if the brand, in general, is important to customers, then, in the minds of consumers, neither the company nor the brand has close substitutes. Therefore, the demand is inelastic.

3. Urgency of need. Although products such as medicine or parts for an imported sports car may not be important in absolute

terms, because of the urgency of need, the demand for the company could be inelastic. Convenience chains such as Seven-Elevens or Hop-Ins are enjoying such need urgency based on convenience, which is preferred over relatively lower prices of not so convenient stores.

4. Ease of want satisfaction. If the company's products are dealing with consumer wants that are readily satisfied, then the demand cannot be expanded by lower prices and, therefore, the demand is inelastic. For instance, after the first set of auto tires, very low prices will not stimulate sales for the second set.

5. Impact of total price. If the prices of the product or the store become too high, the customer may be forced to find substitutes; hence, at a certain price level, demand can become elastic.

6. Economic conditions. In a recession, demand is likely to be somewhat price elastic in terms of price increases and somewhat price inelastic in terms of reductions. Consumers may reduce their purchases and look for the best price. They are unlikely to increase their purchases even though the price becomes substantially lower. Thus, in general terms, maintaining the price line may be the best policy in recessions (Samli, 1989). Thus, while demand is elastic when prices are raised, it is inelastic when prices are reduced.

At different times under different circumstances, companies must consider different price elasticities. Particularly during recessions within certain price ranges demand is inelastic. In Exhibit 7-4 (+) signs indicate these areas. While (+) signs indicate inelastic price situations, areas with (−) signs indicate elastic price situations. When the firm is likely to benefit from price reductions in (−) sign conditions, it is likely to be better off by not lowering the price in (+) sign conditions.

The situations discussed above are subject to change. Similarly, economic conditions also change. Thus, many (+) or (−) signs shown in Exhibit 7-4 can change suddenly as well as over time. The firm must understand price volume relationships and how to optimize volume by proper pricing.

NEEDED: PRICE SENSITIVITY

In the final analysis, because price is the key factor that determines how much the firm will earn, grow, and prosper (Winkler, 1990), proactive pricing must be taken very seriously. Proactive pricing is

Exhibit 7-4
Conditions Dictating Price-Level Strategies

	Price Strategy		
	Below Market	Market	Above Market
Low competition	−	+	+
High level of product importance	−	+	+
Urgent needs	−	+	+
Easy to satisfy wants	−	+	−
Total prices are reasonable	−	+	−
Economy is experiencing a recession	−	+	−
High competition	+	+	−
Low level of product importance	+	+	−
Needs are not urgent	+	+	−
Wants are not easy to satisfy	+	−	−
Total prices are too high	+	−	−
Economy is experiencing a boom	+	−	−

Source: Samli, A. Coskun. 1989. *Retail Marketing Strategies*. Westport, CT: Quorum Books.

closely related to market sensitivity. Sudden and important changes in the economy, which are causing turbulence, require a firm to be market sensitive. Customer needs and changes in life styles are leading toward mass customization, which further necessitates market sensitivity. These are some of the key forces making proactive behavior of the firm necessary.

However, the firm's traditional pricing practices are relatively insensitive to anticipated or actual demand changes because pricing decisions are made without measuring or closely approximating the demand (Balvers & Casimano, 1990). Furthermore, much of the time pricing decisions are simple and mechanical (almost automatic). These situations lead to price stickiness or price inertia, indicating insensitivity to market changes.

During the decade and a half prior to the writing of this book finance people started playing a very serious role in the firm's pricing decisions. They have their eyes on the cost and often think differently. Knowing how to assemble a clear pricing strategy, how to minimize discounts and maximize profits, when and how to increase prices and, above all, how to be market-sensitive necessitates marketing inputs into a proactive pricing strategy that is essential in turbulent times for the health and welfare of the firm as well as the health and welfare of the economy as a whole (Winkler, 1990). Early measurement of customer behavior by sophisticated as well as follow-up research to determine customers' reactions to prices and price related factors is essential for a proactive pricing strategy (Simon, 1992).

Particularly in economic downturns, because of cash flow problems, the firms are tempted to raise prices. This is not only detrimental to the firm, but, typically, to the economy as well. Even if the firm has some monopoly power, in adverse economic conditions, this power dissipates. The firm must be extremely sensitive to customers' reactions so that the firm will not fall into a trap of raising its prices and losing revenues in large proportions.

SUMMARY

Turbulence in and volatility of the market place necessitate a proactive pricing approach. Traditionally, pricing decisions have been made by either cost plus or demand and supply analytics. Neither one of these approaches truly provides the basis for the needed proactivity. Rather, the traditional approaches lead to price stickiness or price inertia, indicating insensitivity to market changes and turbulence.

Finally, sensitivity to market changes and developments such as mass customization will enable the firm to function well in volatile markets. The firm must consider the needs and abilities of many different markets and must develop a price-to-volume combination that will optimize the total revenues as well as the profits.

REFERENCES

Balvers, Ronald J., and Thomas F. Casimano. 1990. "Actively Learning About Demand and the Dynamics of Price Adjustment." *The Economic Journal* (September): 882–897.

Cannon, Hugh M., and Fred W. Morgan. 1990. "A Strategic Pricing Framework." *Journal of Consumer Marketing* (Summer): 57–68.

Kotler, Phillip. 1991. *Marketing Management*. Englewood Cliffs, NJ: Prentice-Hall.

Lancioni, Richard A. 1991. "Pricing for International Business Development." *Management Decision* 29: 39–41.

Lynn, R. A. 1967. *Price Policies and Marketing Management*. Homewood, IL: Richard D. Irwin.

Maital, Shlomo. 1991. "The Profits of Infinite Variety." *Across the Board* (October): 7–10.

Pope, Norwood W. 1989. "So Long Eighties: Bring on the Nineties." *Bank Marketing* (December): 20–21.

Samli, A. Coskun. 1989. *Retail Marketing Strategies*. Westport, CT: Quorum Books.
Simon, Hermann. 1992. "Pricing Opportunities and How to Exploit Them." *Sloan Management Review* (Winter): 55–65.
Winkler, John. 1990. "Marketing Guide: Pricing." *Marketing* (August 9): 17–20.

8

Promotional Decisions in Market Turbulence

INTRODUCTION

Promotional activities gain special importance in turbulent times. In addition to downward economic movement, thousands of small businesses are emerging and major U.S. industries are becoming more oligopolistic. Consumers are not confident of their future, however, and a small group of extremely rich and very large groups of lower income and poor are emerging. In addition to developing promotional programs to counteract the immediate impact of turbulence, the firm must pursue a proactive promotional strategy, which means being aggressive in the market place. This chapter presents a basic outline of an aggressive and proactive promotional program.

THE ESSENCE OF PROACTIVE PROMOTION

In the market place where there are so many different firms, an enterprise cannot automatically establish its identity. The deliberate action to accomplish this identity cannot be too sporadic. Companies, typically, have the tendency to advertise or promote when the economy is in an upswing, and they cut down advertising and promotion in the times of economic slow-down. However, they must continue with their total promotional program and make only a few adjustments at the periphery as the economic conditions change or competitive conditions necessitate.

THE PROBLEM: PAST ORIENTATION

Although it may not be intentional, firms utilize advertising and promotional budgeting procedures that favor past performance rather than present and, particularly, future performance. Exhibit 8-1 illustrates the standard and proposed procedures in managing promotional activity. The key variation between the two approaches is the difference between standard and futuristic orientation in promotion.

Exhibit 8-1
Traditional versus Proposed Promotional Orientation

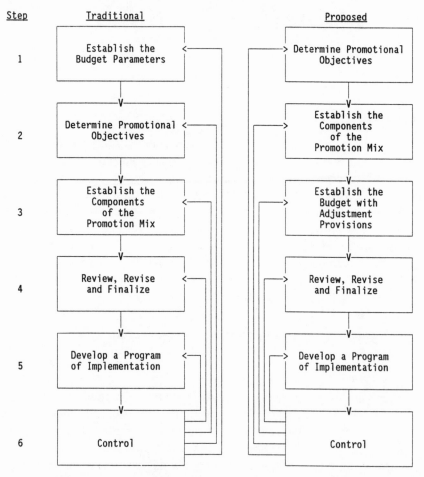

Source: Adapted and revised from Samli, A. Coskun. 1989. *Retail Marketing Strategies.* Westport, CT: Quorum Books.

First establish the budget; then work out its details. Developing a promotional budget and a promotional program are not within the constraints of this book. Any marketing or retailing book will address this issue in detail (see, for example, Samli, 1989).

The critical difference is the place where the budget is developed. The proposed proactive orientation, also called research objective or task objective, is not limited up front by the size of the budget. Exhibit 8-1 shows that the budget in the proactive model is established at step 3 not step 1. The budget that is established at step 3 is based on promotional objectives and the components of the promotional mix. The proactive approach allows the size of the budget to be based on a proactive promotional program. Promotional program comes before the budget is established. Proactivity, here, implies stepping up and changing promotional activities to counteract economic turbulence.

Counteracting Turbulence

Many U.S. companies are trying to counteract a long and prolonged recession. They have started expanding budgets to launch new products and to advertise and promote them. Their thinking is changing in the direction of "instead of just maintaining profit margins, the time is right to think more expansively and grab market share from competitors" (*Wall Street Journal*, October 28, 1992, B1).

This new orientation of increased promotional spending is not uniform. Goodyear Tire and Rubber Company, for instance, increased its national advertising by 30 percent. Many others are changing their promotional outlays, but not at the same proportions.

"Companies that are expanding advertising to support new product launches say they can get more for their dollars when the economy is weak" (*Wall Street Journal*, October 28, 1992, B13). Basically, this is because many companies are still taking the traditional position of financially managing by a bottom line, which means that in adverse economic conditions they become financially more conservative and cut spending.

Seeking a Larger Market Share

Accelerating promotional activity may not be quite adequate to counteract the turbulence. The firm needs to be more proactive within the constraints of a promotional plan that is guided by the promotional objectives. This is why, in Exhibit 8-1 the promotional objectives are shown as the first step. These objectives are further guided by a planned increase in the market share or at least a planned increase in sales. This point is further elaborated in Exhibit 8-2. As seen in Exhibit 8-2, in order to increase the sales volume by about 10 percent, a more than 15 percent increase in promotional activity is necessary. But, an increase of 10 percent in the sales volume makes it possible for the company not to go into red in a deep recession period.

Exhibit 8-2
Increase or Decrease in Financial Statistics
Reflecting Marketing Performance in Turbulent Times
(in percent)

	December 1991–December 1992
Net sales	9.2
Advertising and sales	16.5
Net income	1.1

The most important aspect of Exhibit 8-2 is that the company in question planned to increase its sales volume or capture a larger share of the market in order to combat the negative impact of recession. This planned increase can only be accommodated by the proposed promotional orientation in Exhibit 8-1. Because the budget is based on the promotional objectives as well as the components of the promotional mix, the proposed promotional orientation, unlike the traditional orientation, has the flexibility to accommodate a proactive promotional plan that will more than counteract economic turbulence.

PROBLEM WITH THE TRADITIONAL APPROACH

The traditional model in Exhibit 8-1 illustrates managing by a bottom line as opposed to for a bottom line. Because, much of the time, the total promotional budget is established up front, there is a tendency to scale it down in economic downturns and increase it in economic upturns. This orientation would not allow the firm to fight economic adversities. Once the budget is fixed at the beginning, it becomes quite difficult to be proactive and counteract economic turbulence. Thus, proactiveness in the promotional plan is clearly related to the aggressiveness on the promotional objective and promotional mix as the conditions necessitate.

Because the budget is fixed, the promotional mix and promotional objectives cannot be adjusted to the prevailing market conditions.

The other aspects of the two models are not critical for our purposes here. Typical retailing books would discuss these aspects (see Samli, 1989). However, one point still must be made. The control activity, based on feedback to the question What is happening in the market? (or How well is the firm performing?) must take place swiftly. If the firm has aspirations to increase its market share or increase its sales volume in the middle of a recession, it must follow the impact of its promotional activity closely and it must act fast. If the recession deepens during the promotional activity and the firm does not achieve those goals, an adjustment should be made in the promotional budget as well as the promotional program so that the firm can be adequately proactive and fulfill its promotional objectives.

Howland (1991) aptly makes the distinction between the traditional and proactive approaches. In her words:

Can't afford any "investment spending" right now, you say? Time to focus on cutting back, not growth? The advice of your colleagues is to look up from the ledger and take advantage of the situation. "If you pull back, cut those promotions, fire salespeople trying to save one or two dollars, you may not be able to recover quickly enough when the economy turns around" (p. 58).

These comments depict very effectively the proactive orientation that is a must for survival (and success) in turbulent times. Howland proceeds with a ten-step plan to cope with economic downturns. Although her original comments are related to the publishing industry, they are modified and revised here to make them more applicable to any marketing situation in recessions.

THE TEN-STEP PLAN FOR IMPROVING
SALES IN RECESSIONS

Step 1: Revise Your Selling Practices

In turbulent times businesses must get as close to their customers as possible. This might mean seeing people face to face. Salespeople must reach prospective customers with an approach of "see if we can help." The salespeople need to be more informed and knowledgeable than ever before. More networking, understanding the markets, and exchanging of information in industry association are all necessary ingredients of this orientation. The salespeople have to work faster and harder so that they may stay just one step ahead of competition.

Step 2: Develop a Team Spirit

In order to maintain a high morale, the channels of communication must be open among the salespeople. They must realize that everyone is in this together. There must be a motivational, inspirational dialogue, which is available to all salespeople. The salespeople must realize that they are helping their customers to take advantage of the recessionary conditions prevailing in the market. Therefore, they themselves must understand the real value and benefits of their service to their customers.

Step 3: Develop Joint Promotional Activity

Understanding customers' needs and generating creative activity to solve their problems is also promoted. Just paying lip service to customers' problems particularly in turbulent times will not pay. Joint promotional activity can be very effective in stimulating business.

Step 4: Avoid Being Too Deeply Involved in Special Deals

Although, in recessions, helping the customers to perform better is critical, offering each customer a very special (and mostly unrealistic) deal will confuse the issue. Instead, the salespeople should be given greater latitude to adjust their offers more readily to the customers' needs.

Step 5: More Promotion and Less Image Building

In recessions, the first objective is to survive. Survival under recessionary turbulence is achieved by increasing sales volume as quickly and as much as possible. This is quite different from the conventional thinking of cutting the spending and regrouping (an orientation is referred to as managing for a bottom line in Chapters 1, 2, and 3).

Even though promotional activity typically has a long-term mission of developing an image for the company that will enhance its competitive edge, the value of this activity diminishes in the short run in favor of activities that will stimulate sales. As advertising may promote values, the sales force may concentrate on custom marketing, to sharpen the firm's ability to solve its customers' problems. Through custom marketing, companies truly make themselves valuable and indispensable in the eyes of their customers.

Step 6: Develop Winning Techniques

If there is a time to develop more effective, more informative, and less costly promotional activity, recession is it. A manufacturer, for instance, may develop a system to advertise jointly and effectively with some of its retail customers to develop a total joint appeal to consumers. The company may dig deeper into the businesses of these select retailers in an effort to optimize the results of promotional activity for these clients as well as for itself.

Step 7: Motivate the Sales Force Further

In recessions the typical tendency is to lay off the salespeople. However, this move simply makes the situation worse. Instead, it is extremely important to motivate the salespeople to make them more productive and more dedicated. There may be, for instance, recognition for achievement in the way a presentation is made rather than for an actual sale (Howland, 1991).

Any effort to help the salespeople to understand the problems of customers or end users enhances sales force motivation and effectiveness. If the morale is up, the salespeople perform much better in this area.

Keeping up morale is a formidable task and takes constant diligence (Howland, 1991). Anything from pep talks to assurance of job security is likely to be effective in turbulent times to enhance the salespeople's motivation and loyalty. As this book is written, the author has been exposed to may situations where middle managers and sales force members are so concerned about their own job security that their productivity and effectiveness have come to a halt. Simply being close to the salespeople and working with them as well as reassuring them is likely to enhance the proactivity of the firm as a whole and improve its market position. Thus, enhanced proactivity is partially a function of high morale of the sales force.

Step 8: Don't Lower Expectations

Although demanding the impossible must be avoided, setting sights too low in recessionary times can also be a demotivator. If people feel that not much is expected of them, they may easily adjust their performance to these expectations. Telling someone who sold $1,000,000 worth of merchandise last year that, because of the recession, it is okay if his or her performance is reduced to half may be counterproductive. It would be much better to establish a goal to retain market share or even to gain on this share. This, as opposed to a goal of reducing sales effort or advertising activity, is more positive and constructive. The focus in recessionary times should be on the goal and not on the gloom (Howland, 1991). Selling the sales force on the future is important. After all, recessions do not last forever, and an increased effort today is most likely to pay off tomorrow.

Step 9: Protect Base Salaries and Set Realistic Goals

It is necessary to make sure that the sales force is adequately compensated. However, goals must be realistic. If, in recession, market conditions make it reasonable to achieve a larger market share with a little effort, the goals may reflect that. Adjusted goals should not appear to lower expectations.

Special incentives such as sale of the month, awarded for the best sale — either a new account, a most difficult renewal, the largest new piece of business, or the biggest stretch — can be used successfully (Howland, 1991, 62). Giving plaques, money, or other types of rewards can be used to best advantage in recessions.

Step 10: Take Heart from Successes

If the firm concentrates on creating marketing partnerships with its customers — going after non-traditional ways of stimulating its own business by stimulating its customers' business — and if these approaches work well, then why not thrive on such approaches in times of turbulence? In this way business may weather the storm and gain a larger market share. The travel agent dealing with businesses may find it extremely useful to put the client business in touch with a prospective client business. The two businesses may develop a strategic alliance, and the travel agent may get the travel business of both firms.

From our discussion thus far, it is obvious that businesses must have enough flexibility to counteract economic turbulence with proactive promotional activity.

THE PROBLEMS OF HAVING
"BUSINESS AS USUAL"

Unfortunately, businesses are not quite so flexible. Many firms take the orientation of business as usual. This implies that, once certain plans and financial decisions are made, business continues as usual. The necessary flexibility and proactive behavior are not built into promotional plans. Furthermore, it is assumed that business conditions are not likely to change significantly and that the best approach is to implement the plans as they were originally devised.

This type of conservative and traditional point of view makes it impossible for the firm to cope with turbulence. Many firms can behave this way because they are big and powerful. Therefore, they reinforce survival of the fattest. However, one must realize that by not being proactive and not attempting to counteract turbulence business is likely to lose money in both the present and future. There are two critical reasons for this: business is never as usual and best kept secrets never win.

Business Is Never As Usual

The most important fact that a business should consider about the market is that it is dynamic. Business conditions change under the influence of many short-run and long-run factors. Because no one can be positive as to the direction of market forces and expected changes, business must do the next best thing — maintain a high level of flexibility. Businesses that do not take for granted that what happened last year will happen again and market conditions will not change drastically are likely to perform better.

Since business is not as usual, the promotional plans of the firm should be somewhat similar to a contingency plan. This contingency plan is designed to maintain the proactive orientation of the firm. In Chapter 4, early indicators are mentioned. It is important to connect those early indicators to the performance of the firm and the market conditions. Exhibit 8-3 illustrates the point. As the firm implements its promotional plans, it is extremely important to receive a quick reading on the success of these plans. If numerous external conditions trigger turbulence, it would be futile to stick to the originally planned promotional activity. As indicated in Exhibit 8-3, early indicators of problems or turbulence should activate the contingency promotional plans. These plans, by definition, will reinforce the proactivity of the firm's promotional functions and, hence, counteract turbulence.

Exhibit 8-3
Reinforcing Promotional Proactivity

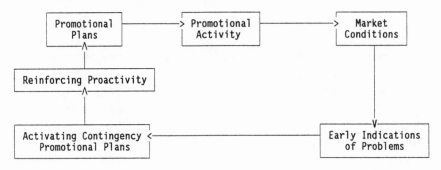

Best Kept Secrets Never Win

Ames and Hlavacek (1989) point out that "it is easier to learn new ideas and approaches than to forget old ones" (19). The traditional orientation to developing promotional plans can actually keep the firm from being recognized as a dynamic, up-to-date provider of consumer utility. The firm, therefore, becomes a best kept secret and a financial robot that reacts belatedly to market conditions and turbulence. This is all caused by not being able to forget old ideas and approaches. Functioning in an extremely dynamic market like a financial robot that is functioning on the basis of traditional rigid budgeting process and not even considering the possibilities of being proactive is totally wasteful and borderline criminal because the firm may lose many of its investors' lifetime savings, not to mention its own lost profits from existing market opportunities. Thus, carefully planned counterturbulence promotion is extremely important for the firm to maintain or improve its market position and maintain a proactive posture. This is an investment. When and if the economy is in a slump, the firm may position itself as favorably as possible for the subsequent recovery and boom periods.

ELEMENTS OF COUNTERTURBULENCE PROMOTION

While the spirit of proactivity is the most essential ingredient, counterturbulence promotion plans must emphasize a minimum of six points: (1) more promotional advertising, (2) more effort to increase productivity of the sales force, (3) more effort to obtain free advertising and public relations, (4) more emphasis on obtaining the same or larger sales, (5) more emphasis on capturing a larger market share, and (6) ability to redirect promotional activity very swiftly.

1. More promotional advertising. Adverse economic conditions must be overcome by activity that will counteract the turbulence. This means a heavier emphasis on promotional advertising that will yield an immediate increase in sales or, at least, maintain the current sales volume. Similarly, if and when the economy takes an upturn, a larger proportion of advertising may be used for institutional advertising to enhance the name and the reputation of the firm.

2. Increasing productivity of the sales force. Although a few comments relating to this concept have been made earlier in this chapter, more needs to be posited. By keeping the sales force morale high, by motivating and compensating the salespeople adequately, and by training the sales force carefully the sales effort can be improved. But, above all, by supporting the sales force with a carefully planned program that will enhance the allocation of the sales effort in the market place and enable the salespeople to solve customer problems in order to satisfy their needs, the productivity of the sales force can be enhanced.

3. Free advertising and public relations. Basically, firms should always be on the lookout to obtain free advertising, publicity, and public relations. An individual firm can accomplish more by being involved in a public service, a news making activity, or public relations. Public relations is particularly important because the firm may be involved in special treatment of some of its customers. That may be a news item. A travel agency, for instance, may have a wish come true program for a very sick child. A hospital may be involved in a ten-K hike to raise money to fight cancer. A bank may sponsor a barbecue to raise money for the local public library. All of these are examples of valuable public relations activities that provide important advertising for the business and cost almost nothing. When a larger budget is needed for promotional activity because of an economic downturn, and if most of the resources for promotional activity are used, then the firm may make a special effort to generate free promotional activity that can be very effective. Perhaps part of the contingency plan that was mentioned earlier can include some of these activities in great detail.

4. Obtaining the same level of sales. In an economic downturn, the firm must at least maintain a certain sales volume. Maintaining the same sales volume or increasing the sales will cost more; therefore, it may be unrealistic to expect greater profits. However, if the firm were to maintain

its proactivity and use the current economic conditions to make an investment for its future, then increased expenditures and reduced profits may be construed to be an important investment for the future. If the firm behaves this way, it will be poised to receive more benefit from the economic upturn than will others who do not behave in the same proactive manner.

5. Capturing a larger market share. Quite closely related to the previous point, the firm, particularly in recessionary turbulence, must try to obtain a larger share of the market. In fact, only by achieving that may the firm be able to remain in the black. Needless to say, once the economic conditions start improving, the profit picture of the firm will improve more proportionately, and the already established competitive edge will pay handsomely.

6. Swift redirection of the promotional activity. In a very dynamic market the firm should not pursue a relatively rigid promotional plan. As is illustrated in Exhibit 8-3, the firm must be able to reinforce its proactive posture by quickly receiving information about the changing market conditions and by activating its contingency promotional plans. Having such contingency plans implies certain learned behavior.

LEARNING CURVE AND PROACTIVITY

Swift adjustments are necessary in the promotional activity so that the proactive status of the firm is maintained, which invariably reduces the losses in adverse economic conditions and more than proportionately increases profits in economic upturns. However, maintaining a continuity in the development of promotional contingency plans is not automatic. It is maintained here that, because of the high turnover rate among company executives, the learning curve, which is the essence of continuity, is not maintained. Typically, young executives, particularly those with finance or accounting backgrounds, think of cutting down expenditures and raising prices. To cut expenditures they streamline advertising budgets and cut down the sales force. These activities, combined with increased prices, create near disaster in recessionary turbulence. The stagflation that took place in the late 1970s was caused by this type of behavior (Shama, 1980; Samli, 1989). The learning curve or knowledge from specific experiences must be put into the contingency plans, and new executives, management trainees, and the next generation of decision makers must understand the importance of counterturbulence promotion and, in general, proactive marketing.

SUMMARY

This chapter posits that promotional activity is extremely important to counteract turbulence. Furthermore, promotional activity is essential to maintain the firm's proactive posture.

Proactive promotion begins not with first establishing a budget but first establishing promotional goals. Establishing components of a promotional mix is the next step. The promotional budget should be flexible. Many firms increased their promotional budgets during the most recent recession. In doing so, firms sought a larger market share or increased sales volume. It may cost more to maintain market share or to increase sales volume; however, this may be considered an investment for the period when economic upturn becomes a reality.

Sales performance needs to be increased in recessions. A ten-step program is presented for that purpose.

This chapter further proposes that the company should not have a business as usual attitude. Business is never as usual, and if the firm remains a best kept secret by not promoting its products and services proactively, it will continue losing ground in the market place.

Finally, counterturbulence promotion must have at least six specific features: (1) more promotional advertising, (2) increased productivity of the sales force, (3) free advertising and public relations, (4) the same level of sales, (5) a larger market share, and (6) swift redirection of the promotional activity. While managements change and new inexperienced managers come to power, what has been learned about turbulence and proactivity must not be forgotten. Provisions should be made for managements not to lose the experiences gained in turbulent times.

REFERENCES

Ames, B. Charles, and James D. Hlavacek. 1989. *Market Driven Management.* Homewood, IL: Dow-Jones-Irwin.
Howland, Jennifer. 1991. "Mining the Recession for Sales." *Folio* (April): 58–62.
Samli, A. Coskun. 1989. *Retail Marketing Strategy.* Westport, CT: Quorum Books.
Shama, Avraham. 1980. *Marketing in a Slow-Growth Economy.* New York: Praeger.
"To Outpace Rivals, More Firms Step Up Spending on New-Product Development." 1992. *Wall Street Journal* (October 28): B1.

9

Customer Loyalty and Total Quality Management in Turbulent Times

INTRODUCTION

Businesses strive for the customers' loyalty in the market place. Those who succeed in achieving this loyalty, almost always establish a competitive edge. Thus, good marketing in both turbulent and calm times revolves around this customer loyalty concept.

In this chapter, the customer loyalty concept is discussed as a counterturbulence measure. It may take different types of efforts to gain and retain customer loyalty in turbulent times. Gaining and retaining this loyalty is part of a deliberate action that is depicted as proactive. It is likely to be achieved by applying total quality management to marketing.

SERVICE IS NOT A PRIVILEGE

Marketing is satisfying consumer needs — providing satisfaction to consumers by solving their problems. In essence, this statement means quality; delivery of this quality is service.

Service for the consumer must not be considered a privilege. All customers are important, and their satisfaction directly affects the well-being of the firm. Well-being of the firm is directly affected by the well-being of the society if that firm considers service a basic right of the consumer rather than a privilege. However, it must also be understood that providing good service not only brings the customers back to the firm again and again but also enhances the society's well-being along with the firm's well-being. As depicted in Exhibit 9-1, the firm benefits from its customers' loyalty and patronage, which are reinforced only by providing them with service and, hence, satisfaction. It is also clear from Exhibit 9-1 that customer satisfaction with the service provided by the firm reflects directly on the society's well-being. Hence, the firm can improve its performance level in two separate ways. First, by finding out its customers' degree of satisfaction or dissatisfaction, the firm can determine its own effectiveness in delivering service. Second, by determining the degree of satisfaction or by measuring the quality of life in the society, the firm can indirectly determine the effectiveness of its performance or delivery of service. If, for instance, consumers are complaining about the insurance industry's performance in the society, Prudential, Lincoln, or any other insurance company will realize that they may not be satisfying consumers' needs and, hence, they are not effective in delivering their services.

Peters (1989) speaks about the importance of customer satisfaction. He says that it is five times more costly to get new customers than to maintain the existing ones. Thus, by serving its customers well, the firm brings them back again and again, which is doubly profitable since the extra cost of finding new customers is substantially cut. The firms that consider service as their customers' natural right are likely to survive market turbulence. They are likely to succeed under any circumstances.

Exhibit 9-1

The Firm's Relationship to the Society and the Consumer

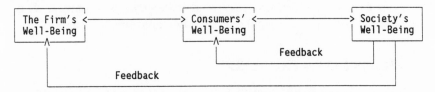

CUSTOMER QUALITY ORIENTED MARKETING

Although good marketing, by definition, is delivering customers quality or serving them, in recent years attempts have been made to equate service and quality and connect all to the company's total being. Tenner (1991), for instance, proposes that a process improvement model can extend quality concepts beyond production and manufacturing into research and development and other non-manufacturing areas. He maintains that process improvement concepts are applied to repetitive manufacturing operations but are not applied successfully to other functions, particularly non-manufacturing areas. Exhibit 9-2 illustrates Tenner's overall orientation. Although this is a general model of the total quality management concept, anybody who is in marketing would recognize that it is also the implementation of the marketing concept. Exhibit 9-2 dwells upon information flow and the company's reaction to information. There are two information flows. First, before production and marketing, information flowing from customers or consumers should form the process to provide the product or service properly to the customer in the way it is required or desired. Second, after production, marketing, delivery, and use or consumption consumers and production (or processing) groups give feedback.

The more closely the firm relates to both of these information flows, the greater is the quality it will deliver to its customers. This quality will serve the customers to satisfy their needs. Thus, quality is service or vice versa. When L. L. Bean, the retailer, correctly ships its orders, including Christmas orders, 99.9 percent of the time, it is displaying quality. If the up time in the production of the Chevy Blazer is 94 percent to 97 percent, that is quality. Xerox adapted various Japanese techniques to cut its unit production costs in half; this is also quality (*Business Week*, November 30, 1992).

Exhibit 9-2
Process Improvement Activity Connecting Consumers to Manufacturing

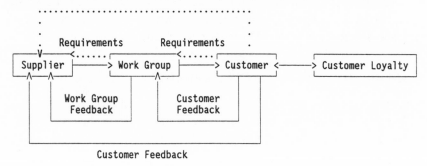

Customer Feedback

NEW CUSTOMERS VERSUS OLD

Bringing in new customers as opposed to dealing with old customers is estimated to be five times more costly. Despite that, marketing typically spends more time and effort in prospecting and getting new customers. Cravens (1988) describes this situation by distinguishing two separate marketing functions: customer identification and customer satisfaction. Customer identification skills are related to assessing the competitive situation, analyzing market potentials, distinguishing different segments and their particular needs, pinpointing target markets, and, finally, developing effective marketing strategies. Cravens believes that this area has traditionally been given the most attention in the marketing literature.

By contrast, customer satisfaction skills have not been cultivated until relatively recently. They have been neglected. This group of skills includes the management and implementation of the marketing program and stresses the importance of the quality and consistency of the marketing process (Parkinson, 1989). This is what Tenner (1991) talks about when he refers to non-production related activities. Cravens et al. (1988) further examine the need for and the development of a total quality management program.

In turbulent economic times, consumers' needs, wants, and desires change. If the marketing activity is primarily emphasizing customer identification rather than customer satisfaction, then as consumers' needs, expectations, and behaviors change, because of turbulence in the economy, the quality that is delivered to the customer is likely to worsen. This will not serve the customers' needs. The opposite is necessary to cope with turbulence. The firm must be proactive in the quality area by providing customer satisfaction. What are the essentials of a customer satisfaction oriented marketing activity? Peters (1989) presents a five-point orientation that constitutes the essence of proactive performance within turbulence: (1) obsession for responsiveness to customers, (2) constant innovation in the firm, (3) partnership among all people in the firm, (4) change oriented leadership, (5) control by simple support systems.

THE ESSENCE OF PROACTIVE PERFORMANCE

Peters' (1989) five points constitute the essence of proactive marketing orientation that focuses on quality and, hence, serving the consumer. It must be posited that the customer in business is not the king; he is everything.

Obsession for Responsiveness to Customers

Peters justifiably focuses on the fact that markets are fracturing. We must, therefore, emphasize specialist rather than thinking mass or volume market (Peters, 1989). The firm, particularly in turbulent times, must create specific niches and differentiate them so that customers identify the company and understand that the company is trying to satisfy their needs totally and completely. Perhaps this point was made in the best fashion by a Japanese executive who said we do not want to just satisfy our customers; we want to delight them (Kotler, 1991).

Milliken and Company, specializing in shop towels (rags), has developed a very customer-oriented, differentiated value adding business. Extremely well trained salespeople have constant access to marketing information, leads, and other assistance through Milliken's data access system. Learning to sell rags and mops, thus, has become almost a science at Milliken. Perhaps the most important aspect of Milliken's business is that Milliken, basically, runs its customers' business for its customers. The company uses the rags sold as an excuse to provide value adding services (Peters, 1989). This kind of proactive behavior is not extreme or a luxury; it is essential to cope with economic turbulence and come out a winner. Peters' formula for this behavior bears repeating:

Make a customer-obsessed revolution. Routinely look at the smallest nuance of the tiniest program through the customer's eyes — that is, as the customer perceives it, not you. Make champions of change in support of the customer, not guardians of internal stability, the new corporate heroes in every function (184).

Constant Innovation in the Firm

The firm, as discussed in Chapter 8, must innovate not only on special occasions but also constantly. The speed of new product or service development must be faster than the changes occurring in the market place that are causing turbulence. The firm must reduce new product or service development cycle times significantly. In doing so, the firm must develop multifunction product or service development teams staffed with full-time people from all primary functions of the firm, for example, design, engineering, marketing, manufacturing, and operations or finance. Outsiders such as suppliers, distributors, and, above all, customers must be involved in this process of new product or service development (Peters, 1989).

Partnership among All People in the Firm

In order to provide quality and serve the customers effectively, all personnel at all levels in all functions must be involved. Quality improvement programs, productivity improvement programs, layout of work areas, assessing new technology, making customer calls, and many other similar programs cannot possibly be implemented successfully without full employee participation (Peters, 1989). If employees are not highly motivated, these programs are likely to fail. Thus, soliciting the participation of all people in the organization and treating them all as partners (and indeed they are) is essential for implementation of proactive plans and strategies. As Peters suggests: "There are no limits to the ability to contribute on the part of a properly selected, well-trained, appropriately supported, and above all, committed person" (284).

Change Oriented Leadership

In order to cope with unexpected turbulence, leaders at all levels must challenge conventional wisdom. They should question the traditionally agreed upon cause and effect relationships. Management must be able to detect the new truths that are not yet clear or must understand them early by being astute students of market changes and the firm's interaction with these market changes.

In a time of turbulence and uncertainty, Peters (1989) posits that the firm must be ready to take action immediately. If such action is to be supported fully, the organization's mission must be clearly understood by all.

If the firm is going to cope with turbulence by managed change, the pact of this change may need to be accelerated. For this, management must show effective leadership by being an example and understanding the impact of its actions on those who are associated with the firm. Additionally, in order to be effective leaders, managers must be compulsive listeners (Peters, 1989).

Control by Simple Support Systems

In every department and in every operation, simple and visible measures must be used to indicate what is important. Developing simple systems that will encourage participation and understanding of everyone is critical. In these systems performance appraisals will continue. The three staples of control over individual — performance appraisals and the setting of objectives and job descriptions — must be redefined or simplified (Peters, 1989). Deming (1986) has maintained that performance appraisal is the number one problem in U.S. management. The same problem can be detected in marketing. The support systems must develop criteria to tackle this critical issue.

These five points, which are construed to be the essence of proactive performance, are the necessary ingredients of quality-oriented managements. The tasks of quality-oriented management might change particularly in turbulent times. Proactive managements can keep ahead of changing conditions by managing change.

TOTAL QUALITY MANAGEMENT IN MARKETING

Companies such as Campbell's Soup, Ford, Hewlett Packard, and Monsanto are, typically, identified as those that accepted and implemented effective quality standards (Parkinson, 1989). In these companies, quality improvements will be a pervasive influence on management thought and practice in the future. "Quality here is defined in terms of the attributes of the physical product or service which the customer receives" (13). Cravens et al. (1988) present two problems creating barriers to achieving quality.

There are two potential quality barriers: (a) the producer may achieve close compliance with the physical specifications of the product which are out of date or otherwise not matched to the customer's needs, and/or (b) the business may not properly determine and adhere to customer desired service standards.

In order to introduce the quality program, Cravens et al. (1988) introduce a three-step process: (1) gain top management's approval, (2) identify relevant marketing process, and (3) evaluate performance.

Gaining Top Management's Approval

Cravens et al. (1988) call this institutionalizing quality improvement. They maintain that, no matter how hard the others might work, if the top management does not approve and commit itself to a total quality management the results will be an exercise in futility. If the whole organization is committed to the concept and concentrates on improving the quality of the business process, then it can not only fight off turbulence easily but also use the turbulence to its advantage. For instance, if the turbulence is recession related, it is known that consumers spend more time comparing prices and seeking lower prices than usual (Cheong, 1991). Thus, the company that has a total quality management program can have more appropriate products produced at lower costs, which automatically will give an advantage to the firm in the market.

Identifying Relevant Marketing Processes

In order to include total quality management in marketing, relevant marketing processes must be used. Among these are: discussion with management to establish its perception of the relevant product and service characteristics; surveys of customers and distributors to determine their perception of the relevant product features; and, most importantly, acceptance and analysis of marketing as a process, along with an identification of its critical elements that are influencing customer perceptions (Parkinson, 1989).

Evaluating Performance

The firm must identify causal factors that may influence the customers' overall perception of quality. By manipulating these factors, the firm can communicate with the markets better and convince its customers of its quality performance. The processes that are being observed must be stable (Cravens et al., 1988). But if there are random disturbances (both internal and external) affecting certain marketing processes, then these processes are not stable. There are a number of techniques that can be used to analyze the stability of marketing processes. If the marketing processes are not stable, the quality cannot be achieved and cannot be served to the customers. Deming's (1986) fifth point posits the following: improve incessantly and forever every process related to planning, production, or service, which implies that proactivity and total quality management thrive on improving the total process through which business is conducted.

Although their writings are applicable to non-service sectors also, Berry, Parasuraman, and Zeithaml (1988), in dealing with the service sector, point out that quality is based on five key areas: (1) tangibles, (2) reliability, (3) responsiveness, (4) assurance, and (5) empathy.

Tangibles

Tangibles include the physical facilities, equipment, and appearance of personnel. If these tangibles appear to be in a specific and proper order, they enhance consumers' service quality assessment.

Reliability

Reliability implies the ability to perform the desired service dependably, accurately, and consistently (Cravens et al., 1988). This is perhaps the most important aspect of quality that influences customers' perception. Cravens et al. (1988) maintain that the most important consideration by the service providers is to deliver exactly what they promised.

Responsiveness

Responsiveness is the willingness to provide prompt service and help customers. The importance of human elements in service quality becomes apparent here. Human performance is extremely critical for customer satisfaction.

Assurance

Assurance is another human element in the service quality arena. It includes employees' knowledge, courtesy, and ability to convey trust and confidence.

Empathy

Empathy is perhaps the most human of the human elements in the service quality area. It implies the provision of caring, individualized attention to customers.

All of the considerations can be put into action in the form of a quality process in marketing. The following section presents one such effort.

QUALITY PROCESS IN MARKETING

Stowall (1989) maintains that although quality improvement techniques are being applied in almost every area of product development, manufacturing, distribution, administration, and customer service they are not well used in many areas of marketing. He further maintains that "few organizations seem to be actively pursuing quality in their marketing functions" (57).

Stowall (1989), quite aptly, maintains that organizations that manage to apply quality to marketing have experienced increased sales and decreased marketing costs. Perhaps, above all, customer satisfaction has been improved.

Stowall (1989) presents a nine-step plan to achieve quality process in marketing. The nine steps in the plan are: understand customer requirements, identify marketing products and processes, match customer requirements to marketing's products, eliminate ineffective products and processes, improve remaining processes, add new processes as required, review the processes for each new product, improve the customer buying process, and involve employees in improving marketing quality. These steps are now briefly discussed.

Understanding Customer Requirements

Marketing revolves around understanding customer requirements. Therefore, understanding customers is a most important step in the direction of success. The firm, in order to fulfill this prerequisite to success, must have answers to questions such as: Who are the customers? What steps do they go through to make a buying decision? What are their key decision factors? Where do they receive their information? (Stowall, 1989). Detailed discussion of these questions belongs in a standard marketing book. Anyone would have a very good understanding about these questions by reading Kotler (1991) or McCarthy and Perrault (1990).

Perhaps the most important point made here, however, is that not only understanding customer requirements but also anticipating them is critical. Understanding customer requirements is necessary, but in turbulent times they change. As Cheong (1991) comments, customers' behavior patterns change during a recession. A proactive firm can detect these changes extremely early. The earlier the firm can detect changes in customer requirements, the greater the chances of not merely coping with turbulence but benefiting from it.

Identify Marketing's Products and Processes

Identification is a controversial area because different people would include different processes in marketing. There are current and futuristic marketing products. Thus, the picture is not clear-cut. Stowall (1989) puts forth a four-point program.

Point One, the planning process. Includes the overall marketing activity. In this case, it emphasizes market research, which translates into information to develop new and improved marketing processes and information products.

Point Two, information development process. Identifies, gathers, and packages data interpreted into information that customers need to make buying decisions.

Point Three, information delivery process. Distributes information to the consumer. Many very involved aspects of the promotional mix development process are included in this point.

Point Four, measurement process. Attempts to determine the effectiveness of the marketing process of the firm.

Match Customer Requirements to Marketing's Products and Processes

This matching combines steps one and two. The marketing information and product development processes must be communicated to the consumer to help them in their buying process. To complete this step effectively, Stowall (1989) suggests that customer requirements must be organized into three categories: the information required, the package in which it is preferred, and the way in which the customer would like to receive it.

Eliminate Ineffective Products and Processes

A natural outcome of the first three steps is the elimination of products and services that are no longer desired and improvement of marketing processes. These activities are particularly critical in turbulent times. Consumers' demands along with their shopping processes are likely to change in economic recession or boom times. These changes can make some products and services almost totally useless over night. If the firm continues producing and marketing these products and services it certainly is putting its existence in jeopardy.

Improve Remaining Processes

Almost by definition, when ineffective products and processes are eliminated, the remaining processes improve. However, each and every process must be improved and must keep on improving. Refocusing on the improvement of effective products and processes clearly improves the firm's chances to survive and prosper.

Add New Processes as Required

The above steps should not lead to self-containment where changes are neither possible nor readily accepted. New processes are likely to come about internally as the production process is improved and as better ways of communicating and dealing with customers are identified.

Review the Processes for Each New Product

The development of new products must lead to the development of new and better processes. Particularly at the beginning, not only the process for production but also the customers' purchase process must be examined and then better marketing processes must be developed.

Improve Customer Buying Process

Customers develop purchase behavior for new products. As this behavior shapes up and as it becomes better understood, the firm can help customers to purchase more easily and solve their problems more effectively. This means improving the customers' buying process.

Involve Employees in Marketing Quality

The detectable decline in quality both in products and services in the United States, during the past decade and a half or so, indicates that all of the stakeholders are not totally involved. The corporate entity has not developed good techniques to involve employees in improving marketing quality. However, techniques, such as productivity teams, quality circles, quality improvement teams, task forces, and corrective action teams, have put much more emphasis on production-related processes than on marketing related processes leading to identifying and satisfying the customer. New and better ways must involve all the employees in all of the activities of the firm. Since they are all stakeholders, they must be allowed to exercise their knowledge of this important fact and act accordingly, which will benefit both the firm and the consumer.

JUST HOW MUCH IS A LOYAL CUSTOMER WORTH?

In competitive markets, success depends on satisfying both loyal customers and potential converts. However, it is extremely important to keep loyal customers satisfied, because it is five times more costly to acquire new customers. When customers are loyal, the new and better products are accepted more readily and the company's success is enhanced. Gillette Company's Sensor razor is one such success story (Mark & Silverman, 1992). The company spent millions of dollars to develop a loyalty-based strategy by developing the Sensor. This is a new removable-blade razor with superior look, feel, and performance. Then Gillette changed its marketing process. It shifted from promotional spending and offering customers price incentives, to media advertising, which builds brand loyalty. Improved quality and processes made Sensor a success story.

Providing customers with a high quality product and service is the marketing concept. Total quality management has been reinforcing this by emphasizing quality in process. As long as the firm is successful in achieving total quality management, the firm will not only overcome turbulence but also benefit from it.

SUMMARY

Creating customer loyalty is the key to counteracting turbulence. In order to achieve customer loyalty, the firm must serve the customer satisfactorily. This can be achieved most effectively by applying total quality management to marketing.

Not only the production process but also the marketing process need to be constantly improved. Evaluating performance is critical to determining satisfaction of a firm's regular, loyal customers.

Finally, a nine-step plan is presented to implement total quality management in marketing: understand customer requirements, identify marketing products and processes, match customer requirements to marketing's products, eliminate ineffective products and processes, improve remaining processes, add new processes as required, review the processes for each new product, improve customer buying processes, and involve employees in improving marketing quality.

REFERENCES

Berry, L. L., A. Parasuraman, and V. A. Zeithaml. 1988. "The Service Quality Puzzle." *Business Horizons* 31(5): 35–43.

Cheong, K. J. 1991. "Recession Retailing." *Retail Control* (September): 3–5.

Cravens, David W. 1988. "Gaining Strategic Marketing Advantage." *Business Horizons* 31(5): 44–54.

Cravens, David W., C. W. Holland, C. W. Lamb, and W. C. Moncrief. 1988. "Marketing's Role in Product and Service Quality." *Industrial Marketing Management* (November): 285–304.

Deming, W. Edwards. 1986. *Out of the Crisis.* Cambridge, MA: Massachusetts Institute of Technology, Center for Advanced Engineering Study.

"The Key to Growth for Small Companies and for America, Quality." 1992. *Business Week* (November 30): 66–75.

Kotler, Phillip. 1991. *Marketing Management.* Englewood Cliffs, NJ: Prentice-Hall.

Mark, Jonathan I., and Jeremy H. Silverman. 1992. "How Much Is a Loyal Customer Worth." *Across the Board* (May): 36–39.

McCarthy, E. J., and W. Perrault. 1990. *Marketing Management*. Homewood, IL: Richard D. Irwin.

Parkinson, Stephen T. 1989. "Management Update." *Journal of General Management* (Spring): 9–16.

Peters, Tom. 1989. *Thriving on Chaos*. New York: Alfred A. Knopf.

Stowall, Daniel M. 1989. "Quality in the Marketing Process." *Quality Progress* (October): 57–62.

Tenner, Arthur R. 1991. "Quality Management Beyond Manufacturing." *Research-Technology Management* (September-October): 27–32.

10

Logistics in Turbulent Markets

INTRODUCTION

Counteracting turbulence, both in the short run as well as the long run, is at least partially related to logistics decisions. Among many aspects of logistics, a few are particularly important in this respect. Inventory controls and financing, distribution efficiency, risk absorption through sourcing and partnering, and value added warehousing are all key aspects of counterturbulence logistics. This chapter presents a discussion relating to all of these logistics issues and connects them to economic turbulence.

INVENTORY CONTROLS

Economic fluctuations clearly influence consumers' needs and desires for products. During a recession consumers become more cost conscious; they prefer cheaper and more products for the money. Typically, they postpone purchasing big items. They try to get more for their money. Similarly, in boom years consumers become more venturesome; they risk more in trying new and more expensive products. They purchase big ticket items such as consumer appliances, automobiles, and homes. Without proper inventory controls, the marketers will either have overages of certain products or underages of others. If these overages and underages are not in the right direction, then the company is bound to lose during turbulent times.

Similarly, markets change, or different markets clearly have different unique desires and tastes. If, again, the inventory control system cannot cope with these changes and differences, the company is likely to lose a lot of money.

Benetton, for instance, an international textile retailer and supplier, found that it must recognize many of the small but important national differences in taste, yet it must rely on its corporate sense of color and Italian design. This behavior pattern on the part of Benetton greatly enhanced its international image of affordable style for aspiring yuppies (Stopford & Baden-Fuller, 1990). Benetton supported this particular proactive orientation with an extremely effective logistics plan. In order to keep ahead of the competition, Benetton decided to have small stores with no wasted space. The company, unlike its competition, developed its capabilities to replenish its inventories. It has particularly fast moving lines during a fashion season, faster than anybody in the trade. Benetton learned to find the fabric, cut it, stitch it, and ship it at a pace probably ten times faster than its competitors. Perhaps the most important key to this successful logistics performance was the company's ability to disseminate information to facilitate its extremely efficient logistics activity.

This logistics activity provides the choice the customer wants at the time the customer desires it. Thus, creating a special customer loyalty enables the company to counteract the negative and at times devastating impact of economic downturns. Similarly, this type of proactive behavior provides the first opportunity to take advantage of economic upturns.

Implied in the above scenario is a sensitivity to changing customer needs and promptness in making those products and services available to customers. Such a sensitivity needs to be enhanced in turbulent times. Maintaining an overall high level of sensitivity enables the firm to be proactive enough to reduce the risks of turbulent market conditions.

Shama (1980) analyzed a large set of data in order to determine the impact of 1976 stagflation on consumers. He identified seven factors that will change the customers' purchase behaviors. The firm can utilize these findings to implement close inventory control and identify logistic needs. If these needs are known early, the firm can be more proactive and, hence, improve its chances to survive and prosper in volatile economic conditions.

1. shopping and budgeting, which is concerned with comparison shopping, bargain hunting, and managing money more carefully;

2. car and car repair, which includes three highly related variables: driving less, putting off car repairs, and attaching high value to fuel economy in cars;
3. economic and political attitudes, relating to loss of faith in the economy and government;
4. purchasing and spending, which is concerned with having to buy less of everything, and at the same time to save more;
5. product variety, which includes consumer perception of product variety, and reluctance to take chances with new products;
6. bills and checkups, relating to paying bills late and putting off medical and dental checkups; and
7. leisure time, which centers on the impact of stagflation on leisure-time allocation: spending time at home, visiting family and friends, watching television or reading, and spending time on do-it-yourself projects (97).

All of the seven factors above indicate first and foremost a very close monitoring of economic conditions and customers' changing moods. Once these are monitored, then inventory adjustments must take place swiftly and effectively.

INVENTORY FINANCING

Potential problems always arise from investments in stocks that do not produce justifiable returns. As consumers' moods and economic conditions change, there will be an accumulation of slow-moving stocks that is, in essence, a very costly proposition for the firm. There should be an on-going policy of reducing any pools of slow-moving stocks that may occur as economic conditions change or turbulence becomes more acute (Scott, 1989).

Computerized, efficient systems are necessary to identify the activity levels of stocks, so that the monies tied up by dead stocks can be minimized. Such dead stocks emerge because of at least three factors (Scott, 1989):

1. Obsolete or inferior quality products or raw materials can cause a gradual build-up of dead stocks.
2. Any damaged or out-of-specification materials left in stocks can cause the emergence of dead stocks.
3. Possible proliferation of brands, types, colors, and design modifications can also cause accumulation of dead stocks.

These situations can emerge because of short-term turbulence or long-term major economic and market changes. In either case, if the business drains its cash resources by investing in ever-growing dead stocks, it may run a risk of using up its financial resources and possibly discontinuing or failing. In addition to a sophisticated inventory system, individual products' contribution margin levels may indicate if dead stocks are emerging. If the products that have a very small contribution margin to the firm's profits are accumulating in the firm's inventory holdings, then this may be considered an early indication of the development of dead stocks. However, sensitivity to customer needs in turbulent times should be considered to be a modifier here. If there is an economic downturn, the profit contribution margin of all products may need to be adjusted downward. This is due to selling products, which means greater value to consumers at lower prices. Among other changing consumption patterns, consumers in economic downturns hunt for bargains, manage money more carefully, and become more economy minded.

Extreme sensitivity to changing customer needs and its resultant economic benefits to the firm cannot materialize unless proper distribution efficiency is exercised. The following section dwells upon this point.

DISTRIBUTION EFFICIENCY

The Milliken & Company example illustrates the importance of distribution efficiency. Like many textile companies in the United States, Milliken was facing very keen competition from low-priced imports. In order to survive and prosper, Milliken used a competitive weapon of high quality logistics (Novich, 1990). The company cut its turnaround time from six weeks to one week and increased its on-time delivery from 75 percent to 95 percent. Thus, Milliken managed to retain its old customers and attract new ones.

Because competition is keen and there are many close substitutes to choose from, manufacturers cannot rely on quality improvements and competitive pricing alone to create and maintain a competitive edge. Hence, they are including superior logistical service as a critical component of their competitive strategy.

Good logistics, therefore, is part of good service to customers and an integral component of overall competitive strategy. Logistics in this case, in Novich's terms, includes "timeliness and reliability of deliveries, ease of placing orders, accuracy of shipments and so on. Defects in these logistical services are as critical to customers as product defects" (1990,

48). Although from strictly a production or cost perspective, logistics may not be more than 10 percent, in terms of reaching customers and serving them, it is much more important than this percentage indicates.

Customers place a very high emphasis on service because its cost can equal or exceed the actual purchase price if logistics services are poor. In a hospital setting, for instance, even though manufacturers maintained a delivery service level of 90 percent, the hospital's total cost of handling the materials, such as tubing and intravenous bags, and dealing with service-related problems more than doubled the total purchase cost of products (Novich, 1990).

As can be seen from our discussion thus far, logistics goes beyond distribution efficiency. It is one of the core concepts of quality and customer satisfaction. In this sense, Ackerman (1989) brings about an additional and important aspect of logistics as he discusses value added warehousing.

Ackerman (1989) maintains that there are important value added services that go beyond the basics of logistics and are of special value to the user. Among value added warehousing functions are packaging related tasks, specialized operations, services adding appeal, and revolutionary services.

Packaging Related Tasks

Packaging products for shipment to the end users is one of the most important value added services. Much of the time, shipping the merchandise in bulk and packaging adequately in the warehouse are not only cost efficient but also value adding. In the warehouse more specific packaging can be performed. Certain specific packaging would be better suited to the needs of different end users and, therefore, add value to the product.

Specialized Operations

Among specialized operations which provide added value in warehousing are: changing the form of the product, reassembling the product, changing temperature for preservation, and performing additional marketing functions (Ackerman, 1989).

If, for instance, furniture is shipped to a regional distribution center in pieces, final assembly might be done at the warehouse. This will save freight costs.

Reassembly may take place to correct a production problem. If, for example, automobile motors are shipped to the warehouse, and if there is a quality problem with carburetors, the carburetors may be changed without returning these motors to the factory.

Changing temperature for preservation takes place in cold storage facilities. Blast freezing is being offered by cold storage operators. The products are frozen for preservation at the warehouse rather than at the factory. The temperature may be changed to control when bananas may ripen, for example.

In some distribution centers, customer telephone orders may be handled. In other cases, funds are collected at the warehouse when products are shipped These are among many marketing functions that are performed.

Services Adding Appeal

There are many reasons why third-party services are appealing. Among these perhaps the most important reasons are leased labor and leased capital equipment (Ackerman, 1989). These are not only cost efficient measures but also may be an opportunity to use the most up-to-date equipment and most effective (or skilled) labor.

Revolutionary Services

Value added services by warehouses are becoming so important that many new and revolutionary services are expected to emerge. Particularly in edible products or those products that are subject to contamination, the packaging operation may be taking place more and more in warehouses. These are important cost-saving activities but necessitate very close inspection and supervision. As goods are shipped over longer supply lines, the importance of value added services at the warehouse level is likely to increase. Therefore, many new and revolutionary services are expected to emerge. All of these add value to the product at the warehouse level (Ackerman, 1989).

One of the most recent value added services by warehouses is sequencing. Parts are received in the warehouse, picked, bar-coded, and sequenced into a unit rotation order prior to delivery for manufacturing. In this way, parts are inspected and quality-tracked. Through sequencing, quality is improved, inventory is reduced, and productivity is increased. As a result, costs also are reduced.

OTHER VALUE ENHANCING COST EFFICIENT MEASURES

The dynamic marketing environment is constantly giving rise to additional arrangements and innovations that are value enhancing and cost efficient. Among these, three are discussed briefly: single sourcing, partnering, and collaborative marketing. These three concepts may overlap somewhat at the periphery, but at the core they mean significantly different concepts or processes. However, it is maintained here that they may create a chain reaction.

Single Sourcing

As external pressures through competition or market turbulence become more noticeable, companies may start establishing stronger relationships with their suppliers, and may enter into single sourcing arrangements. Unlike single sourcing, mainly a cost-cutting arrangement for the buyer, here we are considering late blooming single sourcing that, in addition to supplying some major products or components to the buyer, may expand into producing additional products for the same buyer with major design and end user value in mind. These additional late-comer products may have better designs and may provide better fit with the other components that are already being purchased by the buyer. Thus, this consolidation of sources of supplies may prove to be very beneficial to all parties involved, particularly end users. These flexible arrangements have a particular benefit in coping with economic turbulence, because they may be cost efficient and customer satisfaction laden. They are likely to enhance customer loyalty and create necessary price adjustments in economic downturns.

Partnering

Partnering stimulates participation of some of the supporters to share competitive and economic pressures, absorb some of the losses, but, above all, enhance end user satisfaction. Partnering is done with various suppliers for various reasons. It is, however, proposed here that partnering along with single sourcing is likely to make a more synergistic combination. Value added service for the end user by single sourcing and partnering may be more proportionately enhanced than having only partnering or only single sourcing.

Collaborative Marketing

Collaborative marketing is an old new concept (Magrath, 1991). It has been utilized on and off many times by many companies. In recent years, much has been said about collaborative efforts of old foes like Ford and Mazda or IBM and Apple. Magrath (1991) distinguishes three types of collaborative marketing: product development that involves competitors, simple licensing arrangements between two related entities, and product category sharing that provides an opportunity for more rapid new product development. However, collaborative marketing can also be in any of the functional areas of marketing, such as advertising, logistics, promotion, or selling (Magrath, 1991). Airlines, hotels, and car rental companies have been entering collaborative partnerships. Procter & Gamble co-promoted Pepto-Bismol with H&R Block's tax preparation service by suggesting that each of these companies could play a part in reducing the stress of preparing income tax.

Thus, a chain reaction can be seen among single sourcing, partnering, and collaborative marketing as illustrated in Exhibit 10-1. As the firm moves downward on the partnership path, sharing pressure with suppliers, loss, absorption, and end user satisfaction enhancement all lead in the direction of providing greater resilience, which the firm needs in turbulent times. The enhanced resilience will enable the firm to survive and prosper.

Exhibit 10-1
Partnership Path and Turbulence

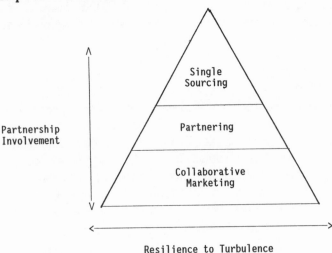

Advancement of Partnership Arrangements

Third-party specialists provide value added services as well as shar-ing pressure, absorbing losses, and enhancing end user satisfaction (Goldberg, 1990). One such company is Customized Transporta-tion, Inc. (CTI) of Jacksonville, Florida. CTI uses its expertise to inte-grate value added services with standard logistics services for its customers. Such a company has much broader experience in trans-portation and distribution than a typical manufacturer. CTI employs technology that its client companies are not able to implement (Goldberg, 1990).

DEVELOPING A GOOD LOGISTICS
SERVICE PROGRAM

Developing a good logistics service program is a major component of overall proactive marketing orientation. Exhibit 10-2 presents a five-step program development process. Following these five steps should enable the firm to take advantage of logistics and value added services, enhance its customers' satisfaction, and, therefore, improve its resilience against turbulence.

Exhibit 10-2
Developing a Good Logistics Service Program

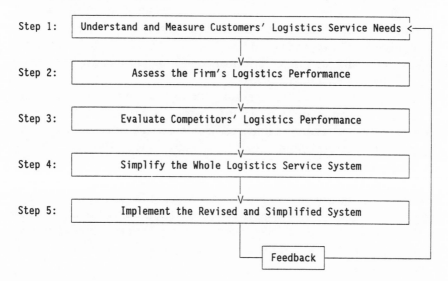

Step 1:	Understand and Measure Customers' Logistics Service Needs
Step 2:	Assess the Firm's Logistics Performance
Step 3:	Evaluate Competitors' Logistics Performance
Step 4:	Simplify the Whole Logistics Service System
Step 5:	Implement the Revised and Simplified System
	Feedback

These five steps are:

1. Understand and measure customers' logistics service needs. It is obvious that understanding and particularly measuring customers' logistics needs is a most critical starting point. If the firm fails to understand and measure its customers' logistics needs, it cannot deliver quality service.

2. Assess the firm's logistics performance. It is extremely important that the firm be in a position to evaluate its own performance objectively. If this performance cannot be assessed effectively, it will not be compared to customers' needs and it will not be possible to identify the areas that need to be improved. There are numerous ways of assessing the firm's performance, although this subject is not within the boundaries of this book. Two groups of assessment measures can be identified. One group is related to cost or input and output relationships, and the second group is related to customer attitudes. Both groups of assessment measures have their own merit, and it is not advisable to choose one over the other arbitrarily.

3. Evaluate competitors' logistics performance. The firm, by definition, must compare its own performance to those of its competitors. If it cannot measure its own performance objectively, it may not be able to assess its competitors' performance objectively either. Furthermore, it is important that the firm use the same assessment techniques for both assessments so that objective comparisons can be made.

4. Simplify the whole logistics service system. Simplification of the system is necessary so that it can function better. Providing customer quality cannot be enhanced by making the system more and more complicated. The revisions and simplification direction would come first from comparing the firm's performance with that of its competitors, and second from overall feedback

5. Implement the revised and simplified system. Implementation is the crux of the whole process. If the system is not in place or is not functioning the way it was intended, then not much value can be gained. Implementation procedures need to be assessed separately and must be carefully monitored.

Finally, as is seen in Exhibit 10-2, an ongoing feedback function must be in place for the whole system. If the management is not sensitive about the overall functioning of the system, then it will not be able to install a proactive logistics system that will reduce the firm's vulnerability to market turbulence.

SUMMARY

Emphasizing value added services along with standard logistics functions provides an additional opportunity to the firm to enhance its resilience and minimize the possible negative impact of turbulence.

In recent years, new developments in inventory controls, inventory financing, distribution efficiency, and value added services in warehousing have given firms the opportunity to enhance end user satisfaction.

In addition to the above functions, cooperating with third parties or establishing partnerships has been effective for the firm in sharing pressure with suppliers and absorbing losses as well as enhancing the end user satisfaction. The partnership activity has gone as far as collaborative marketing.

Establishing a good logistics service system necessitates a systematic and sequential process. A five-step process is identified in this chapter: understand and measure customers' logistics service needs; assess the firm's logistics performance; evaluate competitors' logistics performance; simplify the whole logistics service system; and implement the revised and simplified system. Feedback is necessary at each and every step of the total system.

REFERENCES

Ackerman, Kenneth B. 1989. "Value Added Warehousing Cuts Inventory Costs." *Transportation and Distribution* (July): 33–35.

Goldberg, Daniel. 1990. "JIT's Next Step Moves Cargo and Data." *Transportation and Distribution* (December): 1–3.

Magrath, Alan J. 1991. "Collaborative Marketing Comes of Age — Again." *Sales and Marketing Management* (September): 61–64.

Novich, Neil S. 1990. "Leading-Edge Distribution Strategies." *The Journal of Business Strategy* (November-December): 48–53.

Scott, Don. 1989. "Marketing, Logistics and Inventory." *International Journal of Physical Distribution and Materials Management* 19: 26–30.

Shama, Avraham. 1980. *Marketing In a Slow-Growth Economy.* New York: Praeger.

Stopford, John M., and Charles Baden-Fuller. 1990. "Flexible Strategies — The Key to Success in Knitwear." *Long Range Planning* 23(6): 56–62.

11

How Do the Targets Change?

INTRODUCTION

Up to this point our discussion has been primarily related to factors of turbulence both in short term and long term and the firm's reaction by following a proactive strategy in product development, promotion, and logistics. In order for the firm to develop and implement a proactive marketing strategy that would work against turbulence and improve the firm's chances to survive and prosper, the firm must be very successful in identifying its target markets and maintaining proper contact with these targets. However, target markets, just as everything else in the economy, change. As the targets of the firm change, the firm must either make adjustments to cope with these changes or redirect its efforts toward other and newly emerging target markets.

In this chapter we discuss changing targets and newly emerging target markets. If the firm does not understand its targets and it cannot cater to particular needs of these markets, then it can hardly cope with turbulence and expect to survive.

UNDERSTANDING MARKET SEGMENTS

Markets are not homogeneous They are composed of many homogeneous components that are identifiable, measurable, significant, actionable, and accessible (Kotler, 1991). Because these segments are there and because the firm needs to stand out from its competition and be identified by its markets it has to segment.

This orientation is unique to not only product marketers and retailers but also service marketers, such as banks. Schettino (1991) posits that: "Stimulated mainly by deregulation but deeply hurt by the savings and loan scandals and large loan write-offs, banks today are learning the meaning of the word 'competition'" (75). He goes on to say that this grim economic climate, keen competition, and shrinking bottom line forced the bankers to learn how to market their products and services more aggressively just like the packaged goods sector has always done.

As early as 1956, Smith (1956) discussed both product differentiation and market segmentation as being consistent with the framework of imperfect competition. At the time his position gained little attention. Today in comparison with Wendell Smith's time U.S. economy is experiencing a substantially more imperfect competition. This point was discussed in Chapter 4. Hence, product differentiation and market segmentation concepts are more critical today than ever before.

As Schettino (1991) states, the bank must differentiate itself by creating a unique position in the market place, permitting it to tailor specific products to the needs of market segments that are targeted. The same thing can be said for Lamborghini cars, Ricoh copiers, or Bayer aspirin. Thus, he maintains that segmentation and differentiation go hand in hand. If the business firm can segment its market and caters to this market very carefully, it is likely to differentiate itself also. Perhaps segmentation along with differentiation provides the firm with *competitive synergism* that enhances the firm's ability to survive and prosper in turbulence.

GAP VERSUS LIMITED

In order to understand the differentiation and segmentation created by co-existing and generating competitive synergism, GAP and the Limited, two major retail chains are contrasted. Competitive synergism, if it exists, will give the firm a competitive advantage.

Both are successful retail chains. Although during the 1991–1992 recession the Limited stores performed reasonably well, they increased their promotion and reduced their profit in order to remain in the black.

GAP performed even better. It actually prospered during this long and deep recession.

A comparison of segmentation and differentiation strategies of GAP and the Limited is illustrated in Exhibit 11-1.

Exhibit 11-1
GAP versus Limited: A Comparison of Targeting

	GAP	Limited
Trendy	–	+
Faddish	–	+
Current	–	+
Current with classical lines	+	–
Casual	+	–
Appealing to a larger age group	+	–

The Limited is considered to be more trendy than GAP. Basically, the Limited appeals to the younger generation, which follows the trends and fashions. The Limited lines are perhaps slightly more faddish and, again, attract a younger and perhaps a slightly more "now" generation. Similarly, the Limited lines are seen as more current and less casual.

GAP lines are less trendy and almost not at all faddish. They are more classical rather than being current. Even though some GAP lines may be considered current, they still border on classical lines.

Perhaps the most important distinction between the two chains is that GAP deals with more casual lines that have substantially more longevity than trendy or fashion lines. Similarly, GAP deals with a more upscale market segment that appears not to have been influenced by the recession while the Limited's market segment appeared to have been influenced by the recession. Thus, typical GAP customers continued their regular purchase patterns during the recession while the Limited customers cut down their purchases slightly or needed to be stimulated with more advertising and lower prices.

In order to develop a better focus on customers' needs and satisfaction, some marketing thinkers maintain that successful marketers have become nichers (Dent, 1991).

NICHE MARKETING AND BEYOND

Exhibit 11-2 illustrates five stages in marketing. One may claim that the 1960s were, perhaps, the turning point of mass marketing. By using mass production techniques and by using heavy mass promotion, mass consumption was encouraged.

Exhibit 11-2
Marketing Trends

Time (or Era)		Practice
1960s		Mass Marketing
1970s	Increased	Market Segmentation
1980s	Customer	Niche Marketing
1990s	Satisfaction	Individualized Marketing
2000s		Mass Customization
	V	

However from the late 1960s through the 1970s segmentation became the focal point in marketing practice. Segmentation in those days was more generic in the sense that it was single-dimensional one-variable based and extremely pre-conceived, such as the children's market, the geographic markets, or different income markets. Subsequently other more sophisticated segmentation concepts were developed: psychometrics, benefit segmentation, life style segmentation, among many others (Kotler, 1991).

Dent (1991) gives the next stage as niche marketing in the 1980s. Perhaps niche marketing was not as popular in the 1980s as one might suspect, however, the concept became popular during that era and many successful marketing practitioners used it. Niche marketing implies either focusing on a specific and small segment in which the marketer can be a king and preempt competition, or can strictly corner one part of a large segment and again serve its customers well.

For individualized marketing, Dent (1991) gives the following rationale. He posits that, because customer needs are becoming individualized and customers are becoming smarter and more discriminating, individualized marketing in the 1990s became a necessity. The appropriateness of the marketing message, the quality and customization of the product or service, and the depth of personal relationship with each customer necessitated the development of individualized marketing to a competitive edge and particularly to counteract turbulence (Dent, 1991). It appears that in the 1990s businesses are likely to spend more time and money reaching the customers or prospects who have a clear interest in the products or services offered. Business will also spend more time and money cultivating an ongoing dialogue with each of its customers to enhance trust, loyalty, and repeat purchases (Dent, 1991). This total process is supported by a two-way communication loop. The business must constantly inform its customers of the solutions it has for his or her unique problems. Similarly, the customer constantly informs the business of his or her special needs and requirements. The business must meet these highly specific needs better than its competitors so that it can establish a competitive edge and cope effectively with market turbulence (Dent, 1991).

Individualized marketing may be converted to mass customization where the individualized product or service is delivered in mass quantities (Exhibit 11-2). The Japanese auto industry, the travel industry, some facets of the apparel industry, and the banking industry are all equipped to deliver mass customization. Many other industries are likely to go in this direction. For example, the auto industry is experimenting with the idea that the customer, by identifying certain features in a car, may design a car that is most suited to that individual's needs.

MASS CUSTOMIZATION IS STILL CLOSELY RELATED TO SEGMENTATION

One of the major points Dent (1991) makes is that, to support individualized marketing and mass customization, a computer data base is required. By developing and maintaining key information about each and every customer, the business can efficiently and effectively target specific products and services to those who particularly need them. This data base provides information on the key attributes of customers, and develops composites of target customers based on various combinations of these attributes. These composites are segments, targets, and niches. Although the emphasis is on collecting relevant information about customers, segmentation niching and targeting still remain important. Thus, it is maintained here that the process may begin with segmenting the market and continue on to individualized marketing or mass customization. It is, therefore, necessary to go with specific components of the market that are identifiable, measurable, significant, actionable, and accessible.

However, it is necessary to understand that segments are no longer the same as they were in the 1970s. They are being diffused and more fractionalized. Thus, opportunities are improving for businesses that are developing more finely segmented brands (Mandese, 1989).

CORE SEGMENTS VERSUS PERIPHERAL SEGMENTS

Although, by definition, it is assumed that within a segment there is homogeneity among units, and there is heterogeneity among segments, this homogeneity may be more detectable at the core. For instance, in the elderly market there are certain features that make this segment different from, for example, the teen-age market. According to some the homo-geneity within the market segment is particularly pertinent with respect to the probabilities of selecting different brands in a product class (Grover & Srinivasan, 1989). Grover and Srinivasan (1989) have found that in given segments there are brand loyals and brand switchers. This is consistent with Mandese's (1989) findings: "Among households that use tea, for instance, 82% say everyone uses the same brand today. But that's down from 88% in 1980. Today, 77% of households say they use the same mouthwash which is down from 82%. Colas are 60% down from 68%, and deodorant is 32%, down from 38%" (30). It is obvious that while the core segments remain homogeneous, the brand loyal people at the periphery are switching brands. It also appears that the core segments are shrinking and peripheral segments are growing.

There are two major factors causing this deterioration at the core — secular or long-term trends and short-run trends. Increased individuality in the long run is chipping away the brand loyalty. Similarly, short-run changes, such as economic downturns, would break up brand loyalty as consumers substitute reliability of brand with lower price of substitute products.

The proactive marketer will have to keep a very close eye on the brand power and customer loyalty to the brand. As the loyalty declines and brand switching activity accelerates, decisions must be made to either strengthen the brand or let it coast until it dies naturally. In the meantime, the firm must consider other and more viable alternatives to the weakening current brands.

EMERGING NEW SEGMENTS AND TURBULENCE

As the traditional market segments shrink or change at the periphery, new and critical market segments are emerging. Three of these are briefly discussed here: the mature market, the African-American market, and Generation X.

The Mature Market

This market, or mature populations in general, are especially impor-tant markets because they represent billions of discretionary income (Cutler, 1992). Exhibit 11-3 illustrates estimated increases in different age categories of the mature market. Particularly in the category of 75 years and older, an increase of more than 30 percent is expected.

Exhibit 11-3
The Growth in the Mature Market
                    (in thousands)

Age Group	1990	2005	Percent Change
50+	64.1	84.5	32.0
60+	42.0	47.8	13.8
65+	31.3	35.1	12.0
60+	13.1	17.1	30.7

Source: Cutler, Neal E. 1992. "Myths and Realities of the Mature Market." *Journal of the American Society of CLU & ChFC* (July): 25.

In this fast growing, mature market there are other segments. Cutler (1992) points out that there is more diversity within an older age group than a younger group. He maintains that with maturation comes variation. Some of the mature market members retire while others continue to work; health begins to decline for some while others remain healthy; some become single again.

Elderly consumers have special needs, although these needs are not of equal urgency. This is because the elderly or mature market is not a homogeneous group. In fact it is considered to be a composition of many small segments (Cutler, 1992). However, most elderly, at one time or another, experience these special needs (Samli, 1992). Thus, the marketing practitioner needs to establish his communication system in order to develop enough information about the particular needs of these segments, how these needs must be met, and, of course, how well the needs are satisfied.

One approach to understanding market opportunities is to establish the problem areas that affect the mature markets. Samli (1992) identifies five broad groups of problems: relationship problems, need for special products, need for special services, information needs, and economic problems.

Relationship problems may be connected to family, work, or other social relationships such as club membership, retirement community, and so on. Market opportunities may be in the areas of entertainment, travel, or housing.

Need for special products varies from special foods to special apparel and to specially designed homes and furniture. Any and all of these categories pose a true challenge to proactive marketers.

Need for special services is primarily related to self image (Dychtwald, 1989). Certain services that will provide an opportunity for the elderly to make a contribution to their own self worth are necessary. Certain volunteer services, charitable organizations, and promotional activities featuring the elderly and their contributions to society need to be generated.

The second group of services is related to medical and health care. The elderly's medical and health care needs are rather different and in some cases more intensified than those of younger people (Samli, 1992). Firms must find ways to generate and deliver appropriate services at reasonable costs for these particular consumers.

Information needs of the elderly market are unique. Because the elderly are attached to their routines and certain ways of performing life functions, communicating with them is not simple. Part of this communication can be achieved through reference groups, the behavior and interaction of which influence the elderly (Samli, 1992). Among these reference groups are siblings, friends, neighbors, and service providers (Sherman, 1989). These cohort groups change, disappear, or are replaced by others over time. Firms must be in touch with this market, particularly to inform the elderly about different product and service options and to help them to stay informed so that they can make good purchase decisions (Samli, 1992).

Economic problems of the mature market are very real. Even though the elderly may have substantial wealth accumulated, their incomes, quite often, are limited (Lazer & Shaw, 1989). Firms, in order to gain the broadest possible reach to this segment and the most intensified cultivation of it, must generate reasonably priced products and services. These firms also must find creative ways of financing the older consumers' purchases.

The African-American Market

Although over 31 million African-Americans, who make up more than 12 percent of the U.S. population, may not seem to be as large as some other markets, such as baby boomers (80 million) or the elderly (over 52 million), their number grew by 14.4 percent between 1980 and 1989. This segment spends over $170 billion a year on goods and services (Campanelli, 1991). More and more products that are specifically geared to the black community are introduced to this segment. This market is also composed of different segments based on income, location, or education. The Black Consumer Spending Index shows that black households are 7 percent more likely than any other segment to spend money on food products. The Black Consumer Spending Index also indicates that this market spends 4 percent more than other markets on soft drinks, 7 percent more on cereals and bakery products, 20 percent more on fruits and vegetables, 27 percent more on sugar and other sweets, and 62 percent more on meats, poultry, fish, and eggs.

Almost 99 percent of black households live in rental housing. Blacks are almost twice as likely to buy an expensive foreign model car, such as Audi, BMW, or Mercedes (Campanelli, 1991). There are many other peculiarities to this large and fast growing market. The proactive marketer must find ways to understand these peculiarities, interpret them into needs, develop products and services to satisfy these needs, and market these products and services accordingly.

Generation X

Perhaps the most recent and unique market that is emerging in the United States is named Generation X (*Business Week*, December 14, 1992). This market is almost 46 million strong between the ages of 18 and 29. They are tattooed and pierced. They were the first latchkey generation. They graduated as the economic recession was at its worst. They feel shut out, angry, neglected, and pessimistic about the future. They have strong musical preferences. Their fashions, which are described as post-industrial thriftshop, are composed of flannel shirts, baggy or ripped jeans, teva sandals, and reversed baseball caps.

Thus far, Generation X has been a virtually invisible segment. X-ers have been mostly ignored by U.S. media, businesses, and public institutions. This is likely to change. After all, an annual spending power of $125 billion cannot be ignored. Proactive businesses, particularly in the areas of beer, fat foods, cosmetics, entertainment, and electronics, are likely to reach out to this segment quickly and make substantial progress in making money in exchange for providing satisfaction.

OPERATIONALIZING A PROACTIVE MARKETING PROGRAM

As these new market segments emerge, proactive marketers must target them. This will call for a well planned and managed marketing program such as the one presented in Exhibit 11-4.

Exhibit 11-4 provides the highlights of an effective proactive marketing plan. Like all good marketing plans, it begins at the market. Obviously, if the unique needs and peculiarities of the emerging segment are not

Exhibit 11-4

Proactive Marketing to Cope with New Market Segments

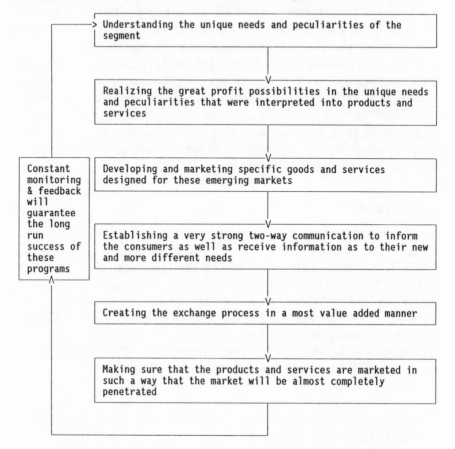

understood, the firm is not likely to make any progress in terms of successfully marketing goods and services designed for this segment.

Once the unique needs are understood they must be interpreted in terms of market opportunities and profit possibilities. This can be achieved by interpreting unique needs and peculiarities into products and services.

The next step in Exhibit 11-4 is particularly important — developing and marketing those specific products and services that are designed for the emerging market segments.

In order to develop and market these new products and services a very strong two-way communication process needs to be developed. The stronger the two-way communication system the more information it will carry both ways. The specific groups of consumers will receive information regarding the newly developed products and services. Similarly, the business will be able to assess the needs of these groups very quickly and adjust its products and services offerings accordingly.

Along with information flow, an exchange process must be created so that total quality management will provide maximum satisfaction. Most of the principles discussed in Chapter 10 are applicable here. Most value added principles need to be considered at every stage of the marketing process.

Finally, the business must make sure that its products and services are marketed in such a way that the market segment will be completely penetrated. This total cultivation of the market is particularly beneficial for the national economy.

Constant monitoring of this total process and development of a feedback system that will guarantee the long run success of these programs is a given, which reinforces the strength of this model. Constant monitoring is essential because the model presented here does not depict a one time transaction but rather a continuing process. The continuity and success of the process depends on this close monitoring and feedback.

SUMMARY

This chapter deals with the markets. Markets change constantly. If the firm cannot cope with these changes it will be devastated in turbulent times. Because markets are not homogeneous, segmentation has become common practice. A five stage marketing evolution has been presented as the starting point for analyzing procedures that deal with the markets' heterogeneity. The five phases of evolution are: (1) mass marketing, (2) market segmentation, (3) niche marketing, (4) individualized marketing, and (5) mass customization. This evolution indicates that, in time, concentration on the individual is still the focal point. However, emphasizing the individual is more within the context of segmentation than randomization.

Market segments, in time, change, primarily at the periphery rather than the core. These changes, along with other effects of turbulence, have a very strong impact on the firm's well-being. A proactive marketing plan, therefore, must include not only the changes that are taking place in the existing market segments but also those segments that are emerging. Three such segments are briefly discussed in this chapter: the mature market, the African-American market, and Generation X.

REFERENCES

Campanelli, Melissa. 1991. "The African-American Market: Community, Growth and Change." *Sales and Marketing Management* (May): 75–81.

Cutler, Neal E. 1992. "Myths and Realities of the Mature Market." *Journal of the American Society of CLU & ChFC* (July): 24–26.

Dent, Harry S., Jr. 1991. "Individualized Marketing." *Small Business Reports* (April): 36–45.

Dychtwald, Kerr. 1989. *Age Wave: The Challenges and Opportunities of an Aging America.* Los Angeles: Jeremy P. Tarcker, Inc.

Grover, Rajiv, and V. Srinivasan. 1989. "An Approach for Tracking Within-Segment Shifts in Market Shares." *Journal of Marketing Research* (May): 230–236.

Kotler, Phillip. 1991. *Marketing Management.* Englewood Cliffs, NJ: Prentice-Hall.

Lazer, William, and Eric H. Shaw. 1989. "Income Assets and Consumption: The Relative Well Being of Mature Consumers." In *Quality of Life Studies in Marketing and Management,* edited by H. Lee Meadow and M. Joseph Sirgy, 265–279. Blacksburg, VA: Virginia Tech.

Mandese, Joe. 1989. "Who Are the Targets." *Marketing and Media Decisions* (July): 29–35.

"Move Over Boomers." 1992. *Business Week* (December 14): 74–82.

Samli, A. Coskun. 1992. *Social Responsibility in Marketing.* Westport, CT: Quorum Books.

Schettino, Anthony M. 1991. "Segmentation Helps Bankers Stand Out from the Crowd." *The Bankers Magazine* (March/April): 75–77.

Sherman, Elaine. 1989. "A Retrospective of Selected Issues Concerning Quality of Life and the Elderly Consumer." In *Quality of Life Studies in Marketing and Management,* edited by H. Lee Meadow and M. Joseph Sirgy, 228–238. Blacksburg, VA: Virginia Tech.

Smith, Wendell R. 1956. "Product Differentiation and Market Segmentation as Alternative Strategies." *Journal of Marketing* (July): 3–8.

12

Value Marketing and Turbulence

INTRODUCTION

AST Research Inc.'s 1991 revenue grew 41.4 percent to $827.3 million. The company's secret is value marketing — making the right product available at the right time and right price. Texas Instruments, Inc.'s revenues grew 6.8 percent to $747.9 million. The company's information technology group and its case tools have been primarily responsible for restructuring business and manufacturing processes throughout the company. Price Waterhouse's worldwide revenues were up 25.5 percent to $733 million because the company made a major effort to keep its costs at 1990 levels and focused on core industries and services. Through acquisitions and alliances, Novell, Inc. established itself as a one-stop source for network operating systems, resulting in a 35 percent increase in 1991 revenues to $710 million. Packard Bell Electronics, Inc. has been pursuing a market penetration strategy that helped the company to achieve gross revenues of $819 million. All of these success stories took place during the 1991 recession (The, Davis, McCusker, & Marks, 1992). Perhaps the common thread among these companies is their effort to serve their respective markets with value marketing. This chapter presents the concept of value marketing as a major counterturbulence weapon. After citing a few examples and establishing the parameters of value marketing, I will discuss the components of value marketing and its impact. Value marketing is very close to the relationship marketing and interactive marketing concepts that are emerging in the recent literature. From a different perspective, value marketing is also closely associated with the most recent concept in the management literature: total quality management.

THE VALUE OF VALUE MARKETING

Value, today more than ever before, has become essential in marketing. Today's consumers want to know what value they are receiving for their money. This may translate into low prices along with other less-tangible value indicators such as lifetime product warranties, added value and discount programs for frequent purchasers, superior customer service, close monitoring of customer satisfaction, and the like (Levere, 1992).

Companies find it necessary to respond to this increased demand for value by developing innovative marketing strategies. However, reactive marketing is responding to demand for value while proactive marketing is detecting the increased demand for value early enough so that the firm utilizes this important change by delivering more and better value swiftly and ahead of competition (Samli, 1992). The more swiftly the firm moves into a situation like this the greater the value it delivers.

Many companies have developed proactive marketing plans based on the demands of increased value. Among these are the Mexican fast food chain Taco Bell. Its value priced menus helped increase profits more than 25 percent while the fast food markets have been extremely flat. Sears KidVantage, a children's apparel program featuring a wear-out warranty and discounts for frequent purchasers, has been received enthusiastically (Levere, 1992).

Taco Bell Experience

Two points explain Taco Bell's success. The first is the value menu. The company's research identified that customers were not happy with the value they were getting for their money. Thus, the whole process of trying to give people more for their dollars started. The company has been trying to maintain the quality of its products while lowering prices (Levere, 1992). The second point is food service and physical appearance of the restaurant. All of the activities, functions, and resources that help the company deliver value to its customers must be reinforced and supported by the management. Everything else is non-value adding overhead.

To implement its strategy, Taco Bell altered roles and responsibilities within the organization. Among these changes were:

1. The number of stores under the direction of one market manager increased from 5 in 1988 to 20.
2. Sophisticated information technology was installed that freed up the manager's time.
3. Managers with the newly freed time doubled the time they spent on staff training.
4. Automating food preparation enabled the staff to focus on customers and their needs (Levere, 1992).

The company observes that the value strategy is not simply a function of price but of revamping the whole company. The increased value through marketing, no doubt, will enhance customer satisfaction and resultant customer loyalty. These conditions, by definition, create a counterturbulence posture for the company that enhances its survival probability and chances of making more money.

Sears

While Sears' everyday low price policy that was launched in 1989 was a failure, its KidVantage program, a multi-faceted apparel program introduced in 1991, appears to be succeeding. Customer research indicates that people who buy children's clothing are motivated by four key factors: value pricing, frequent sales, brand selection, and concerns that kids either wear our or outgrow their clothing too quickly (Levere, 1992). In response to these factors the KidVantage program was initiated. The program features:

1. competitive pricing on all children's clothing;
2. special promotions and sales (such as Kid's Day, back-to-school promotions, and in-store appearances by children's book characters like Winnie the Pooh);
3. an inventory of 70 national brands available in all Sears stores;
4. wear-out warranty; and
5. frequent purchase program.

The warranty enables customers to return merchandise if it becomes worn out while the child still wears the same size. Sears will replace the merchandise free of charge with an identical item or with similar items that represent equal value in the same size group.

For the frequent purchase program, customers receive a special KidVantage card that keeps a record of their purchases, including size, number, and dollar amount of Sears' Kids and More clothing. When customers buy $50 worth of merchandise in the children's department they earn a 10 percent discount on a future Kids and More purchase. A $100 purchase will give them a 15 percent discount (Levere, 1992).

Again, increased value will increase customer satisfaction and customer loyalty. Increased customer loyalty is perhaps the most important insurance against market turbulence. However, the nature and the extent of the value offered may change depending upon the acuteness (or lack thereof) of turbulence.

CUSTOMER SATISFACTION CHALLENGES

Counterturbulence marketing thrives on retaining loyal and satisfied customers. As economic and market conditions change these loyalty and satisfaction concepts are revised so that the firm can maintain its existence and prosper. Band (1989) maintains that "customer satisfaction is a straightforward philosophy" (19). It simply means putting the customer first. He goes on to say that increased productivity, strengthening of distribution systems, or driving for a higher market share are not necessarily putting the customer first. The customer is not king; he or she is everything. Facing the customer satisfaction challenge is the crux of proactive and counterturbulence marketing plans known as value marketing.

Customer satisfaction challenge is reflected by some critical developments in the market place. These are causes of turbulence as well as solutions to it. Among these developments, six are critical and are discussed here. Understanding these critical developments will pave the way toward developing a sound value marketing program. The developments are: uncertainty; time management; market fragmentation and customization; quality, design, and service; responsiveness; and constant improvement through front line personnel. Exhibit 12-1 presents these key developments as factors facilitating the planning of a value marketing plan. These six developments are discussed below.

Uncertainty

As changes take place in the market at an accelerated pace, uncertainty also increases. By definition, increased uncertainty forces the firm to pay more attention to changing customer needs and requirements. Because

Exhibit 12-1
Critical Developments in the Market Place and Value Marketing Implications

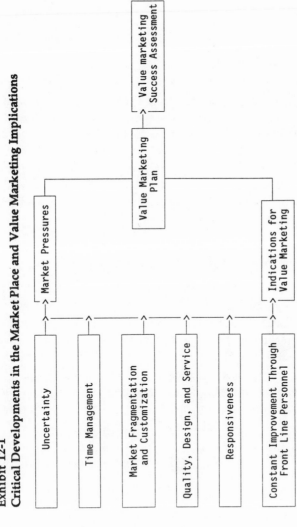

customer needs and expectations change continuously, constant innovation is necessary to adjust to these changes and to reduce uncertainty. The Taco Bell and Sears examples indicate not only the need for but also the advantages of continuing innovation. Royal Bank of Canada, in its attempts to shorten bank line-ups, extended hours of operation and provided more informed personnel (Band, 1989). Although this may appear to be cost inefficient, increased customer satisfaction more than offset this cost factor.

Time Management

In modern, unpredictable, and turbulence ridden markets time has become a competitive weapon. While the changes occur in the market place, those companies that can respond quickly and convert these changes to profitable solutions manage to develop competitive advantage. The firm needs to be timely and must bring new technologies and designs to market. Johnson and Murphy Shoe Company of Nashville designed an automated quick response system in order to improve the processing of shoe orders and make sure that the shoes that are popular and selling well will not be out of stock (Band, 1989).

Market Fragmentation and Customization

Today's customer is better informed, more knowledgeable, and more changeable. Markets are being redefined, fragmented, and, subsequently, customized (Band, 1989). Many major industries, such as hospitality, travel, food, and cosmetics, have been cognizant of these changes and have been customizing their products accordingly. For the hospitality industry, innovations such as non-smoking floors and specially located rooms for business women who are traveling alone, along with exercise facilities and frequent visitor programs, are the type of customization activities which are responses to market fragmentation.

Quality, Design, and Service

In almost all markets more and more customers are pressuring suppliers to add value to their products and services. Superior product quality, innovative design, and value adding services are becoming more readily recognized as the basis for competitive advantage (Band, 1989). The "Quality is Job One" campaign of Ford Motor Company reflects this orientation. Similarly, Toyota advertises the "Toyota Touch," which claims quality products, quality service, and quality salespeople who care for the customer. Toyota backs this claim with a commitment to total customer satisfaction, which is backed by a toll-free number for questions, concerns, or complaints (Band, 1989).

Responsiveness

Oligopolistic forms are gigantic, inflexible, and far removed from markets and consumers. As they emphasize increasing productivity, reducing costs to strengthen their distribution system, or strive for larger market shares they do not put the customer first. Because their decision making mechanisms are far removed from consumers they lack the sensitivity and responsiveness to consumer needs. Band (1989) states that

The General Motors concept of managing large corporations has been proven ineffective. In 1953 Charles Erwin Wilson boasted that what's good for General Motors is good for the country and vice versa . . . but by the 1970s General Motors had become dangerously arrogant and smug . . . blindsided by competitors . . . hamstrung by unmotivated workers and production inefficiencies and outmoded plants (20).

Things have not changed much since then. Unless large companies learn to be more responsive they will eventually lose out.

Constant Improvement through Front Line Personnel

Front line personnel are the closest to customers and the work process. Hence, they have many ideas to increase customer satisfaction and provide continuous opportunity for improvement. It is extremely important that the ideas of the front line personnel are harnessed systematically and regularly.

The six critical developments discussed previously are pressures imposed upon the individual firm through the market. These are also signs or cues as to how a value marketing plan can be constructed. As seen in Exhibit 12-1, the six critical developments create market pressures and also help create a value marketing plan.

CONSTRUCTING A VALUE MARKETING PLAN

In the early 1990s two new marketing terms appeared. The first is relationship marketing — the idea of cultivating a long term relationship that is mutually beneficial (Gill, 1991). The second is interactive marketing — the ability to develop interactive relationships with individual customers (Blattberg & Deighton, 1991). These two concepts are similar if not the same. They also are very close to the concept used in this book — value marketing. Value marketing is generating value through marketing process for the end users in such a way that they will stay with the company.

Although this author has maintained that "any marketing is value marketing" (Samli, 1992, 177) in that marketing always adds some value however optimizing the buyer and seller as well as the society's values requires a major change in the *marketing orientation*. The key points of this changed orientation are shown in Exhibit 12-2. These are individually discussed so that the foundations of a value marketing plan can be laid out. The points are: segmentation, advertising, promotion, pricing, sales management, distribution channels and logistics, new products, and monitoring and feedback.

Segmentation

Traditional approach has been based on demographic and psychographic profiles of current and prospective customers. Similar profiles are grouped and treated identically.

In value marketing, in addition to the traditional approaches, actual behavior patterns are used to identify customers. Then these customers are associated with certain specific addresses and statistical models are used to determine the value of each address. Customers, hence, receive customized offers individually or on tightly identified niches. Mary Kay Cosmetics built a multimillion dollar business selling to women at home parties by using a network of beauty consultants. The turnover of these consultants was extremely high for the company. In 1986 the company started building a data base of its customers. If the consultants supplied the names of customers, each client received a Personalized Beauty Analysis. This analysis consisted of a questionnaire completed by customers about skin type and color, hair color, facial shape, and makeup preferences. Upon the analysis of these data each customer received a diagram illustrating recommendations. This data base, today, contains 9.5 million names. Since 1989 the party plan selling process has been supplemented by five catalog mailings per year. This system provides customers image-enhancing communication to position the firm's products with those of competitors and maintains an ongoing relationship (*Direct*, 1990).

Advertising

Traditionally, mass communications are designed for the target groups as a whole. It has been more supply oriented reflecting the advertiser's point of view.

In value marketing, advertising is based on information about the individual customer. Computer-driven magazine binding makes it possible to insert special messages selectively into print advertising. Other modern methods of communicating with individuals in the market place are also used.

Promotion

Traditionally, promotional offers are inserted in newspapers or magazines or mailed indiscriminantly to various homes. Indiscriminant mailing is based on geodemographics.

In value marketing, however, promotion is much more carefully tailored to individuals' past behavior. This promotion is based on the expected pay-offs from promoting directly to customers. The message is delivered specifically to the individual creating a much tighter communication process between the marketer and the customer.

Pricing

In traditional marketing, products are priced differently for different market segments. These prices are adjusted on the basis of market acceptance or consumer reactions.

In value marketing, however, pricing is more readily based on the knowledge of the individuals, their price sensitivity, and past behaviors. Prices are further adjusted to the individual's ability to pay along with these individuals' value needs or value perceptions.

Sales Management

Traditionally, customer data have been used for the salespeople's own needs. Typically, the data are also kept with the sales group.

In value marketing there is access to customer files by the sales group but the data are housed at the top management level and are also used to fulfill organizational goals. Calling on customers is based on this information. Prospect data bases are tied to call reports that not only would improve sales force performance but also help monitor the sales effort and control its performance.

Exhibit 12-2
A Comparison of Traditional and Value Marketing

	Traditional Marketing	Value Marketing
Segmentation:	Based on demographic and psychographic profiles of current and prospective customers. Similar profile groups are treated identically.	Using actual behavior patterns to identify customers and statistical models to determine the value of each address. Customers receive a customized offering individually.
Advertising:	Communications are designed for the target group as a whole. It is more supply advertising reflecting the advertiser's point of view.	Using information on individual customer. Computer-driven magazine binding allows selective insertion of print advertising. Other modern methods of communicating individuals directly are also used.
Promotion:	Special promotional offers are inserted in newspapers or magazines or mailed indiscriminately to homes based on geodemographics.	Are tailored to an individual's past behavior, are based on the pay-off expected from promoting to the consumer and delivered solely to that individual.
Pricing:	Products priced for different market segments and adjusted based on market acceptance or consumer reactions.	Pricing takes place on the basis of the knowledge of the individuals, their price sensitivity and adjusted to the individual's ability to pay, keeping individual's value needs or perceptions in mind.

Sales Management:	Customer data tends to be housed with the salespeople, who use it as needed to enhance their own goals.	There is access to customer files and can use them to achieve organizational goals. Targeted calling programs are based on these files. Prospect data bases that are tied to call reports improve salesforce monitoring and control.
Distribution Channels and Logistics:	The organization depends on intermediaries and direct selling from a salesforce to reach customers. Warehouse transportation and other logistics activities are all purely cost driven.	The firm is directly linked to the customer. Intermediaries join in but do not take over. Logistics activities are value added driven and optimize the end-user satisfaction.
New Products:	Research and development is driven by the firm's technology and production systems, somewhat isolated from the market conditions.	New products and services are designed based on the company's affinity with the customer.
Monitoring and Feedback:	Market share, sales, and profit are the critical tools to monitor performance. Reviews are periodic and usually annual.	Traditional measures are supplemented by early signals in the market. Success in retaining customers and cost of acquiring new customers are measured. Customer satisfaction is approximated often.

Source: Adapted and revised from Blattberg, Robert C., and John Deighton. 1991. "Interactive Marketing: Exploiting the Age of Addressability." *Sloan Management Review* (Fall): 12.

Distribution Channels and Logistics

Traditionally, the organization depends on intermediaries and direct selling from a sales force to reach customers. Warehousing, transportation, and other logistic activities are all purely cost driven.

Value marketing implies that the firm is directly linked to the customer. Intermediaries join in but do not take over. Logistic activities are all value added driven (see Chapter 10) and optimize the end-user satisfaction.

New Products

New products in traditional approach are substantially more research and development and technology driven. The firm's production system has had more to say on new product decisions. Therefore, new product decisions are somewhat isolated from the conditions and realities of the market place.

Value marketing emphasizes new products and services that are designed to enhance the company's relationship with its customers. Loyal customers are served by outsourcing or by the company's own resources. The critical point is that loyal customers' needs dictate the new product development process (Blattberg & Deighton, 1991).

Monitoring and Feedback

Traditionally, market share, sales volume, and profit have been the critical tools for monitoring overall performance. Periodic reviews, usually annual, are used for adjustment.

In value marketing, traditional measures are either supplemented or substituted by early signals in the market. Success in retaining the current customers and cost of acquiring new customers are measured. Customer satisfaction is measured or at least approximated often. The value of the existing customer base is monitored on an ongoing basis.

Value marketing requires some significant attitude changes toward marketing processes. However, Exhibit 12-2 does not really specify the specific steps involved in a value marketing plan.

PUTTING IT ALL TOGETHER

Perhaps what Nieman-Marcus, Waldenbooks, and Brooks Brothers are doing in recent years, along with many other companies, indicates what value marketing is about. All of these firms are, according to Gill

(1991): "enticing customers to remain loyal by adding value to their credit cards or creating purchase incentives for a core customer group" (39). These proactive marketing plans, which are providing end users with greater value, may take many different shapes but they are composed of numerous basic features. A few of these were pointed out earlier by Samli (1992) in a different context.

At least nine critical features must be considered in order to construct a value marketing plan that will be proactive and counterturbulent. These features are: (1) offer products that perform; (2) give more than the consumer expects; (3) give guarantees; (4) add more value; (5) avoid unrealistic pricing; (6) give consumers the facts; (7) build relationships; (8) penetrate the market; and (9) monitor, monitor, monitor. A brief discussion follows below. This section draws heavily from Samli (1992).

Offer Products that Perform

Of course, the concept also includes services. There is performance and there is performance. Since the product or service is a bundle of utilities (Kotler, 1991), offering a product that performs implies satisfying the customers' needs and providing the customers with optimum quality. Because better performance means more satisfaction and more satisfaction leads to customer loyalty this is almost a given as a counterturbulence measure, except that in different turbulent times performance of the product may be perceived differently. While a highly durable but reasonably well performing product may be acceptable at one point in time, in another point in time better performance at a higher cost may be more acceptable.

The same considerations are applicable to services. The proactive philosophy here should not be "give them any color they want as long as it is black" or simply "satisfy the consumers' needs" but it should be "let's delight out customers." In order to delight the customer, the firm must offer a very good product or service.

Give More than the Consumer Expects

Attempting to delight the consumer through a value marketing plan goes beyond offering a good product or service. There must be a plus factor that the consumer did not even think of receiving. These may be frequent buyer programs, gifts with purchase that are given directly at the point of purchase or redeemed by mail, or contest sweepstakes and other related concepts that give consumers a real chance to win something by mail (Levere, 1992). There are many other factors such as environmentally sound packaging, including air conditioning in the car's standard price, free special delivery, and the like.

Give Guarantees

Offering an enhanced and comprehensive warranty and paying full refunds without delay are critical features of a value marketing plan. Again, this aims at delighting the customers and gaining their loyalty. These are not cost factors but safety factors against turbulence and translate into future profits. Thus, these features are an investment for the future.

Add More Value

When logistics issues are discussed many value added functions are brought to the fore. As value adding functions are performed end users or customers will benefit from the cost saving and value generating activities of the whole process. Thus, a value marketing plan must be supported with a value adding logistics function. These two, together, can provide the firm's customer with the best value possible.

Avoid Unrealistic Pricing

Companies should not think in terms of profit per unit. Charging premium prices may not be justified by the product. Furthermore, if pricing was intended to maximize the utilization of the firm's total productive capacity and, hence, optimize profits by selling the largest possible volume, not only the firm will receive handsome returns on investment but also customers will receive great benefits from buying reasonably priced products. Depending upon the intensity or the nature of turbulence the price must be adjusted in the direction of gaining and keeping customer loyalty.

Give Consumers the Facts

Provide consumers with valuable information that will enable them to make important purchase decisions through advertising, promotion, labels, packaging, brochures, and so on. These decisions will increase the value received. Both today's sophisticated customer and today's confused customer need help to improve their purchase decisions and particularly to feel good about them. Therefore, they literally demand factual and detailed information about the products and services they are considering buying. Developing sharper and better functioning communication systems are extremely critical for value marketing.

Build Relationships

Relationships mean additional customer value that translates into repeat sales. This means added customer loyalty (loyalty toward the product, brand, or company). Good marketing means repeat sales and repeat sales are an important counterturbulence measure. Any and all such devices as frequent buyer plans, 800 numbers for additional product information, and membership clubs can help develop product and brand loyalty.

Penetrate the Market

No matter how small or big the target market is, it is necessary for the firm to use its production and distribution facilities fully. Therefore, special efforts must be made to capitalize economies of scale and economies of scope. Not only the products that work but also the products that are wanted, needed, and desired must get into the hands of those who want, need, and desire them the most. This means effectiveness in distribution and logistics above and beyond efficiency (Samli, 1992). The increased effectiveness enhances the value generated and delivered by marketing. As long as there are excess capacities in production, distribution, and logistics, the firm is in a more vulnerable position. It may not be able to cope with turbulence. The firm, therefore, must penetrate the market to a point at which not only those who are at the core of the market but also those who are at the periphery of the market will receive these products and services. When there is more for everybody at a reasonable profit, the firm is counteracting turbulence rather vigorously.

Monitor, Monitor, Monitor

If customer satisfaction is the acid test of value marketing, then, there must be a constant monitoring activity. Among other means of monitoring, a customer satisfaction audit (CSA) is necessary (Band, 1989).

Companies must systematically determine the strengths and weaknesses in their current strategies for delivering high levels of customer

160 COUNTERTURBULENCE MARKETING

satisfaction to enhance their competitive edge and ensure against turbulence.

The customer satisfaction audit is a sound data base to enhance the effectiveness of value marketing. It may include four separate data bases: management climate survey, employee opinion survey, customer satisfaction survey, and internal client survey (Band, 1989).

1. Management climate surveys determine the degree to which the top and middle management are aware of and responsive to customer needs. They also may indicate how well the management is managing the company. Elimination of internal problems through such surveys can be the first step toward improving the management's ability to concentrate on customer priorities.

2. Employee opinion surveys tell supervisors and managers what the employee morale is like and how that may be improved. If employees are not satisfied, they are not motivated, and, therefore, they cannot deliver value to customers.

3. Customer satisfaction surveys can take different forms. Opinions of customers can be carefully analyzed regularly, or customer surveys can be taken randomly. Customer complaints can be carefully registered and investigated. Finally, customers who, after the first time, drop out and never go for repeat purchases may be investigated.

4. Internal client surveys are useful to determine how different departments in the business respond to each other's needs as a function of the company as a whole. Interdepartmental conflicts must be eliminated so that, again, employees can focus on customer requirements (Band, 1989).

SUMMARY

This chapter emphasizes the importance of value marketing as the most important counterturbulence device. A number of examples of such proactive marketing plans are presented.

In order to maintain loyal and satisfied customers the pressures created in the market place must be understood. Six critical developments are discussed as market pressure generating factors. These are: uncertainty; time management; market fragmentation and customization; quality, design, and service; responsiveness; and constant improvement through front line personnel. These factors also indicate some of the basic features of a value marketing plan. Value marketing, as opposed to traditional marketing, reflects some major changes in the management's attitude. We analyzed these attitude changes.

Finally, the key features of a value marketing plan are discussed. A proactive and counterturbulence marketing plan, value marketing in this book, has nine key features: (1) offer products that perform; (2) give more than the consumer expects; (3) give guarantees; (4) add more value; (5) avoid unrealistic pricing; (6) give consumers the facts; (7) build relationships; (8) penetrate the market; and (9) monitor, monitor, monitor.

REFERENCES

Band, William. 1989. "Are You Ready for the Customer Satisfaction Challenges of the 1990s?" *Sales and Marketing Management in Canada* (December): 19–20.

Blattberg, Robert C., and John Deighton. 1991. "Interactive Marketing: Exploiting the Age of Addressability." *Sloan Management Review* (Fall): 5–14.

Gill, Penny. 1991. "Added Value." *Stores* (October): 39–40.

Kotler, Phillip. 1991. *Marketing Management* Englewood Cliffs, NJ: Prentice-Hall.

Levere, Jane L. 1992. "The Value of Added-Value." *Incentive* (Part 2), (May): 18–21.

"Mary Kay, Avon Augment Salesforces with Databases." 1990. *Direct* (September): 24.

Samli, A. Coskun. 1992. *Social Responsibility in Marketing*. Westport, CT: Quorum Books.

The, Lee, Leila Davis, Tom McCusker, and Don Marks. 1991. "The Datamation 100: AST Research, Inc.; Texas Instruments, Inc.; Price Waterhouse; Novell, Inc.; Packard Bell Electronics, Inc." *Datamation* (June 15): 99–106.

Epilogue

U.S. markets are going through turbulent times. The chances are that this turbulence will not subside, rather it is likely to intensify. Firms must learn to cope with this turbulence if they want to survive and prosper. Survival in the market place begins and ends with successful satisfaction of ever-changing customer needs. The firm must be able to develop proactive and counterturbulence marketing strategies to improve its chances of survival and success.

This book posits that the firm can not only survive turbulence but also benefit from it. It all depends upon the firm's overall market orientation and the satisfaction it can deliver to its customers. Counterturbulence marketing, therefore, is not just a passing fancy or a figment of imagination but truly a must in today's challenging business world.

Value marketing is the proposed tool for the firm to cope with the dynamic nature of its markets. This concept is discussed in some detail. Furthermore, the conditions that are necessary for the development of a value marketing plan are articulated to a certain degree. It must be understood that every firm has the opportunity to develop its own value marketing plan and implement it successfully. Different sections of this book delve into the process that would enable the firm to develop a value marketing plan. If this process is not followed carefully an effective value marketing plan cannot be planned and implemented successfully.

A five step process enables the firm to sharpen its capabilities to develop a value marketing plan. Exhibit E-1 illustrates this five step process. Although various chapters in this book discuss these steps in

Exhibit E-1
The Five Step Process to Facilitate the
Development of a Value Marketing Plan

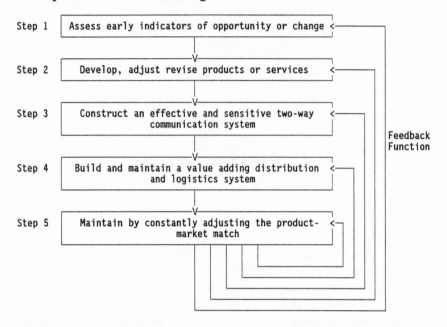

greater detail, the steps must be reviewed here so that we may establish the blueprint for future marketing.

THE PROCESS TO FACILITATE
VALUE MARKETING PLANS

The five step process is as follows:

Step 1

The firm must be cognizant of turbulence and key changes in the market place that are likely to threaten its existence. Furthermore, it must be capable of translating these changes into market opportunities.

Step 2

The firm's products and services must not be looked upon as an end but a means to an end. The end is survival and prosperity; the vehicle is the firm's products and services. As market conditions and opportunities change the firm's offering (product service mix) must be on top of this change.

The firm must revise, adjust, and delete its existing products and services and innovate new ones almost immediately.

Step 3

A two-way communication enables the firm to understand its customers' needs, wants, and aspirations, as well as their degree of satisfaction with the firm's overall offering. At the same time, the firm can inform its customers almost individually as to changes in the existing products and services as well as new products and services that are developed.

Step 4

The firm must be in a position to distribute its goods and services to its particular customers (effectiveness of the distribution system) at the lowest possible cost and highest possible value (efficiency of the distribution system). Thus, the distribution and logistics systems take on a meaning of their own. Marketing and logistics are not substitutes. They must co-exist, collaborate, and, above all, be customer satisfaction oriented so that the firm can be a successful value marketer.

Step 5

The success of value marketing depends upon the tightness of product-market matches. If the firm has very tight product-market matches, it means that its products are very well liked and accepted by its particular target markets. Thus, a firm's customers are loyal and repeat their purchases. This situation is the best insurance against market turbulence. However, particularly in turbulent times, the product-market matches may need much closer adjustment as often as possible.

It is obvious that the five step process, which enables the firm to become a successful value marketer, thrives on feedback. At each and every step there must be feedback indicating proper performance and a smooth overall process. If major or minor adjustments need to be made, the feedback system will indicate how and why. If these adjustments are processed successfully, feedback will indicate what else may be needed for further improvement.

Although this five step process appears to be simple and straight-forward, most firms are not quite capable of putting it into action. The management must be in a marketing mode.

MANAGEMENT'S ORIENTATION

U.S. management has become unduly bottom line oriented. If the firm is forced to manage itself by a bottom line up front, it will never have the opportunity to become a value marketer because up front bottom line constraints will never allow the firm to develop the five step process to facilitate the development of a value marketing plan. The budgetary constraints that are imposed on the firm at the beginning will restrict its marketing performance later. Thus, financial management is not the best means to fulfill the firm's goals and protect it from turbulence. The firm must not be managed by a bottom line. Rather, it must do whatever is needed to achieve a bottom line. It must be managed for a bottom line. This latter implies also, and perhaps most importantly, counterturbulence marketing and, therefore, success as a value marketer.

It is obvious that if the management does not have a value marketing posture, the firm cannot practice counterturbulence marketing. Its chances for profit loss, actual loss, discontinuance, or failure, therefore, increase. If the firm develops a value marketing mode it must have a research agenda.

RESEARCH AGENDA FOR VALUE MARKETING

Value marketing is based on understanding the changes in the market. Thus, the first and foremost research activity is to have a market audit that will determine the critical changes in the market place and how they translate into market opportunities.

Product research has to be carried out at two separate levels: market driven current product research and market driven futuristic product research. Both research activities are very tightly market driven because they are guided by the values, attitudes, and behaviors described by consumers.

Communications research is particularly important because the markets are being fractured and individuals are becoming more discriminating in their needs and purchases. Communications research, which will pave the way for better communication with the firm's customers, is a must for future value marketing.

Distribution and logistics research are even more important than the market audit, product research, and communications research because they are cost and efficiency driven. Much cost savings, along with value added, will materialize if distribution and logistics research takes place on a continuing basis.

Finally, creative research techniques need to be developed to determine the tightness of the product-market matches that the firm utilizes. Because this is the crux of value marketing the degree of tightness and its comparisons with industry averages and competitors can be most valuable. Feedback research must go on in all phases of the five step process.

PUBLIC POLICY TOWARD MARKET TURBULENCE

Public policy toward economic or market turbulence is an extremely critical area of discussion. Because the general emphasis here has been on the firm and its counterturbulence marketing strategy public policy decision aspects are not emphasized.

The cost of turbulence to the society and the firm is so high that counterturbulence public policy issues must be carefully researched and discussed. This topic has not been discussed extensively. It may be quite reasonable to develop a research agenda specifically dealing with this area of interest. The research agenda at the beginning should be in the form of who, how, what, and why.

Who Should Be Involved in Public Policy Counterturbulence?

Public policy counterturbulence research may be pursued at two separate levels, federal and local. At the federal level, information needs to be gathered leading to skills that are critical to providing direction to local authorities in the area of counterturbulence. In this context, at the federal level the following information, among others, needs to be accumulated:

intensity and nature of turbulence to indicate, for instance, the length and depth of a recession or a boom;

regional analysis of the turbulence to determine if it is impacting more or less in different regions;

nature of local impact to examine the local vulnerable spots that would have a major economic impact. For instance, the local industry is the appliance industry. A deep recession is likely to hurt that industry more than others.

macro counterturbulence measures to establish local consulting services for small businesses, developing a financial system that will spread out the burden of recession rather than allowing it to concentrate; and

guidance and information for local authorities to establish a strategic information system that the local public administrators can call to receive specific guidance and information.

At the local level, business leaders, along with public administrators, may develop economic plans that would nullify, if not totally eliminate, the negative impact of turbulence. It is, for instance, quite possible to observe local businesses that are at the verge of failure, not because they are not run well, but because of turbulence. Local leaders may be able to establish a safety zone for such businesses, which may enable them to postpone paying immediate bills and receive free advertising and even free business consulting from a locally established committee of experts.

How Should Counterturbulence
Public Policy Be Developed?

All communities have some type of economic development agency. It is important that these or similar agencies be beyond the economic development issues and take the economic pulse of the community. In doing so, this particular group, or a similar group, may initiate the implementation of certain local counterturbulence plans.

What Should Be Included in the
Counterturbulence Plans?

If the turbulence is negative and economic conditions are worsening, then the counterturbulence measures must be such that the businesses that are negatively impacted may be given some measure of relief in terms of finances, promotion, and guidance and consulting.

If the turbulence is in the form of a boom, the local plans should take advantage of newly emerging opportunities as swiftly as possible. There may be guidance for new businesses to get started, for others to expand in different directions, and to take measures against an expected and forthcoming economic downswing. This latter may include local economic diversification to strengthen some of the weak local businesses.

Why Should There Be Counterturbulence Public Policy?

It is very important to reiterate, time and again, that economic turbulence is extremely costly to the society as a whole and local economies in particular. If turbulence is not counteracted or stopped, communities, as well as the nation, are likely to suffer great economic losses.

Much research is needed to help businesses develop counterturbulence postures. Public policy officials must be in a position to understand the need for cooperation with the private sector in this all-important area.

Selected Bibliography

Abell, D. F. 1978. "Strategic Windows." *Journal of Marketing* (July): 21–26.

Ackerman, Kenneth B. 1989. "Value Added Warehousing Cuts Inventory Costs." *Transportation and Distribution* (July): 33–35.

Alderson, W. 1965. *Dynamic Marketing Behaviors*. Homewood, IL: Richard D. Irwin.

Ames, B. Charles, and James D. Hlavacek. 1989. *Market Driven Management*. Homewood, IL: Dow Jones-Irwin.

Band, William. 1989. "Are You Ready for the Customer Satisfaction Challenges of the 1990s?" *Sales and Marketing Management in Canada* (December): 19–20.

Bennett, R. C., and R. G. Cooper. 1981. "The Misuse of Marketing: An American Tragedy." *Business Horizons* (November-December): 51–61.

Berry, L. L., A. Parasuraman, and V. A. Zeithaml. 1988. "The Service Quality Puzzle." *Business Horizons* 31(5): 35–43.

Campanelli, Melissa. 1991. "The African-American Market: Community, Growth and Change." *Sales and Marketing Management* (May): 75–81.

Cravens, David W. 1988. "Gaining Strategic Marketing Advantage." *Business Horizons* 31(5): 44–54.

Cravens, David W., C. W. Holland, C. W. Lamb, and W. C. Moncrief. 1988. "Marketing's Role in Product and Service Quality." *Industrial Marketing Management* (November): 285–304.

Cutler, Neal E. 1992. "Myths and Realities of the Mature Market." *Journal of the American Society of CLU & ChFC* (July): 24–26.

Deming, W. Edwards. 1986. *Out of the Crisis*. Cambridge, MA: Massachusetts Institute of Technology, Center for Advanced Engineering Study.

Dougherty, Deborah. 1990. "Understanding New Markets for New Products." *Strategic Management Journal* 11: 59–78.

Drucker, Peter F. 1980. *Managing in Turbulent Times*. New York: Harper & Row.

Drucker, Peter. 1989. *The New Realities*. New York: Harper & Row.

Dychtwald, Ken. 1989. *Age Wave: The Challenges and Opportunities of an Aging America.* Los Angeles: Jeremy P. Tarcker, Inc.

Hise, Richard T. 1991. "Evaluating Marketing Assets in Mergers and Acquisitions." *Journal of Business Strategy* (July-August): 46–51.

Howland, Jennifer. 1991. "Mining the Recession for Sales." *Folio* (April): 58–62.

Hulbert, J. M., and E. T. Norman. 1977. "A Strategic Framework for Marketing Control." *Journal of Marketing* (April): 12–20.

Keynes, John Maynard. 1936. *The General Theory of Employment Interest and Money.* New York: Harcourt Brace and Company.

Kotler, Phillip. 1991. *Marketing Management.* Englewood Cliffs, NJ: Prentice-Hall.

Lancioni, Richard A. 1991. "Pricing for International Business Development." *Management Decision* 29: 39–41.

Levere, Jane L. 1992. "The Value of Added-Value." *Incentive* (Part 2) (May): 18–21.

Linneman, Robert E., and Harold E. Klein. 1985. "Using Scenarios in Strategic Decision Making." *Business Horizons* (January-February): 64–74.

Magrath, Alan J. 1991. "Collaborative Marketing Comes of Age — Again." *Sales and Marketing Management* (September): 61–64.

Maital, Shlomo. 1991. "The Profits of Infinite Variety." *Across the Board* (October): 7–10.

Mark, Jonathan I., and Jeremy H. Silverman. 1992. "How Much Is a Loyal Customer Worth." *Across the Board* (May): 36–39.

"Mary Kay, Avon Augment Salesforces with Databases." 1990. *Direct* (September): 24ff.

Naisbitt, John. 1982. *Megatrends.* New York: Warner Books.

Naisbitt, John, and Patricia Aburdene. 1990. *Megatrends 2000.* New York: William Morrow and Co.

Novich, Neil S. 1990. "Leading-Edge Distribution Strategies." *The Journal of Business Strategy* (November-December): 48–53.

Ohmae, Kenichi. 1982. *The Mind of the Strategist.* New York: Penguin Books.

Peters, Tom. 1989. *Thriving on Chaos.* New York: Alfred A. Knopf.

Phillips, Kevin. 1991. *Politics of Rich and Poor.* New York: Harper Perennial.

Samli, A. Coskun, and Tansu Barker. 1984. "Early Diagnosis of Marketing Problems." *Management Forum* (March): 22–26.

Samli, A. Coskun. 1992. *Social Responsibility in Marketing.* Westport, CT: Quorum Books.

Samli, A. Coskun, Kristian Palda, and A. Tansu Barker. 1987. "Toward a Mature Marketing Concept." *Sloan Management Review* (Winter): 45–53.

Schettino, Anthony M. 1991. "Segmentation Helps Bankers Stand Out From the Crowd." *The Bankers Magazine* (March/April): 75–77.

Schnaars, Steven P. 1987. "How to Develop and Use Scenarios." *Long Range Planning* 20(1): 105–113.

Shama, Avraham. 1980. *Marketing in a Slow-Growth Economy.* New York: Praeger.

Shapiro, Isaac, and Robert Greenstein. 1991. *Selective Prosperity.* Washington, DC: Center on Budget and Policy Priorities.

Sherman, Elaine. 1989. "A Retrospective of Selected Issues Concerning Quality of Life and the Elderly Consumer." In *Quality of Life Studies in Marketing and Management,* edited by H. Lee Meadow and M. Joseph Sirgy, 228–238. Blacksburg, VA: Virginia Tech.

Simon, Hermann. 1992. "Pricing Opportunities and How to Exploit Them." *Sloan Management Review* (Winter): 55–65.

Stopford, John M., and Charles Baden-Fuller. 1990. "Flexible Strategies — The Key to Success in Knitwear." *Long Range Planning* 23(6): 56–62.

Tomasco, Robert. 1990. *Downsizing: Reshaping the Corporation for the Future.* New York: American Management Association.

Weston, J. Fred., and Kwang S. Chung. 1990. "Takeovers and Corporate Restructuring: An Overview." *Business Economics* (April): 6–11.

Winkler, John. 1990. "Marketing Guide: Pricing." *Marketing* (August 9): 17–20.

Zarnowitz, Victor. 1990. "A Guide to What Is Known about Business Cycles." *Business Economics* (July): 5–13.

Index

ABOUT THE AUTHOR

A. Coskun Samli is a Research Professor of Marketing and International Business at the University of North Florida in Jacksonville. His most recent books include *International Marketing* (1993), *Social Responsibility in Marketing, Retail Marketing Strategies*, and *Marketing and the Quality-of-Life Interface* (Quorum 1992, 1989, 1987). He is the author or co-author of more than thirty other booklength studies and over two hundred articles in the field of marketing. Dr. Samli was a Ford Foundation Fellow, Sears AACSB Fellow, Fulbright Distinguished Lecturer, and AACSB Beta Gamma Sigma L. J. Buchan Distinguished Professor. He has done numerous projects and consulting work in the areas of business failures, small businesses, and entrepreneurship.